Thank goodness you're here!

Written and illustrated by Suzy Cooper

PO Box 395 Lenah Valley, Tasmania, Australia, 7008
www.suzycooper.com.au

Copyright © Suzy Cooper, 2022

ISBN: 978-0-6454291-1-4

A catalogue record for this book is available from the National Library of Australia.

Self-published March 2022

The moral right of Suzy Cooper to be identified as the author of this work has been asserted.
All rights reserved.

No part of this publication may be reproduced, stored in or introduced into a retrieval system,
or transmitted in any form or by any means (electronic, mechanical, photocopying, recording or
otherwise), without the prior permission of both the copyright owner and the publisher of this book.

Publisher: Suzy Cooper, 2022 (www.suzycooper.com.au)

Editing: Mel Roome at Hit Send (www.hitsend.com.au) – any mistakes are the author's own

Book design: Julia Dineen Design (www.juliadineendesign.com.au)

Hello

The world
needs more
thinking people
like you to get
their bums
onto seats at
tables where
decisions are
made.

"Thank goodness you're here!"

'Politics needs people with brains and hearts bigger than their egos'

Perhaps you've been looking at the people who make decisions on your behalf and thinking, 'We deserve so much better than this.' If you think it's time for people with values like yours to be part of the decisions made in your neighbourhood, school, local council, committees and boards, state or federal government – I've written this book for you.

You might find that you can become a decision-maker simply by putting up your hand or applying. That's terrific. However, you may have your eye on an elected role – requiring people to vote for you – but you have misgivings or don't know where to start.

This book is for you if you're a thinking person who's thinking of standing for an election, and you're:

- ambivalent about politics in general or about your election in particular

- freaking out a bit, or a lot

- not willing to do the stereotypical politician-y things you 'ought' to be doing (kissing hands and shaking babies)

- thinking there must be another way to do it – a way that allows you to keep your self-respect, not sell out, not spend hours banging on doors or desperately trying to 'get media'

- struggling with some of the real but not-to-be-underestimated things that might block you (worried about your hair? worried about things from your past that might become public?)

Let's find your ways of campaigning that won't need you to sell your soul or sacrifice friendships. You can expand your comfort zones bit by bit.

I'll give you a few different ways to think through, design and run your own election campaign using methods that suit your personality. I'll also address some realities about what might get in the way – for you and for anyone thinking of voting for you – and how to handle them.

"Thank goodness you're here!"

1

By and large I'm aiming this book at someone who might want to run their entire campaign themselves. However, if you're thinking of running for a state or federal election, you'll probably be employing a team of people and recruiting or managing volunteers. Nevertheless, you might find my ideas for contacting people in personal and creative ways still work better for you than using mass media.

If you read this and decide that the role of decision-maker isn't for you, or isn't for you right now, but you know someone who'd be great at it, hopefully you'll use some of these ideas to help with their election campaign (if you want to). Or you might decide to lend your support to someone who's already in a decision-making role and be in a position to contribute your own ideas. There are lots of ways to change things.

'If you don't intend to do politics like everyone else does, then don't campaign like them.'

The things I'll suggest in this book aren't rules, they're suggestions. I want you to question everything and figure out how to run your campaign YOUR way.

My good news for you:

- You can start exactly where you are, with who you are.

- Even introverts (actually, maybe especially introverts) can run amazing election campaigns.

- Running a campaign and trying to get elected can make you, and everyone you talk to, feel more powerful and hopeful.

I know because I did it successfully myself.

I hope that just reading this book will open up new possibilities about making a difference, whether or not you run a campaign or get elected.

"Thank goodness you're here!"

Come on. Let's go.

"Thank goodness you're here!"

"Thank goodness you're here!"

What do I know about getting elected?

Hello. I'm Suzy Cooper.

This book isn't about me – it's about you.

I want to help you to get elected because I want to see more real human beings making decisions in our schools, neighbourhoods, towns and countries.

I believe that you can make changes on all kinds of scales if you stick with your values, find the people who yearn for the things you want to see more of, get into conversations with them, offer and accept help, enjoy some laughs and collectively throw your shoulders behind something worthwhile.

What do I know about this election business? Well, I got myself – a complete political unknown – elected to an Australian capital city council with some unusual – but effective – communication tools. They suited me and they suited the prospective voters I was talking to. You can see what I did, and why, in Chapter 7: Anatomy of my campaign.

I used what I've learned in over 20 years as a communications consultant to work out what was important to me (my messages), who I thought might share my values and vote for me (my audience), and how I might reach them. I did things that fitted my personality and values, and some that just felt like fun.

4

You and I have only just met, but I'm betting that, since you've picked up this book, you're interested in being a different kind of decision-maker and running a different kind of election campaign.

I'll address the confronting bits of the whole process and provide you with ways to create your own campaign in manageable pieces, without being boring or sounding like a stuffed shirt.

We can work out your ways of campaigning to get you into the minds and hearts of the people who might vote for you, while keeping yourself nice. And by 'yourself' I mean your values, sanity and bank balance. By 'nice' I mean not waking up with regret-sweats.

I'll share my thinking and provide prompts so you can decide what you do or don't want to do, and how you might do it to suit the kinds of people who'll be voting for you.

This icon lets you know there are downloadable templates to help with particular aspects of planning your campaign. Find links to these templates in the Handy Templates section.

So, go forth. Find some great people, come up with good ideas, do things you get a kick out of and get yourself elected. Democracy needs your brain, your voice and your energy.

suzycooper.

Chapter 1

You

"Thank goodness you're here!"

Why you?

That's a big question, isn't it? Don't go foetal or hide under the stairs – it's really normal to have 'Aaargh' feelings, even about things you want to do.

If you're not sure about your underlying motivations for wanting to become a decision-maker, then here's a small exercise to help you burrow into them.

Getting clear about the things that drive you, your basic values, can help you decide whether things are opportunities or distractions.

Your 'Why' can form the basis of the messages, platforms or policies you use in your campaign.

Exercise – Why do you want to do this?

Grab the scrappiest bit of scrap paper you can find to write on – at least A5 size. You'll throw it away after you get to the good bit.

1. Write down the reason you want to stand for this election.

2. Now write down why that reason is important.

E.g. I want to stand for this election because we could make some big changes if we replaced the snoozers doing the job at the moment.

Now answer the question Why for every answer you write, until you think you can't go any deeper.

Why do I want to replace the snoozers? Because they don't represent the people in our community, and they make decisions that suit people just like themselves.

Why is representation important? Because we miss out on lots of good ideas and also it's not fair if some parts of the community don't get things they need.

So there's something about fairness there. And something about valuing good ideas that come from a range of places.

"Thank goodness you're here!"

Maybe, for this example, you could summarise the underlying values as:

'I want to see good/different ideas that are fair for everyone in the community considered by this group of decision-makers.'

What have you come up with?

Stick your summary statement to your wall somewhere you'll see it all the time. This will remind you why you're doing this.

I know I said you were going to throw it away.

That was a trick to get you to take the pressure off when sidling up on this valuable exercise. OK. You're allowed to rewrite what you learned onto a nicer piece of paper.

However, that scrappy piece of paper might remind you of the scrappy person who started out on this idea in the first place. There's beauty and truth in the imperfect.

What you've written is one of your values. You might use this in your campaign as an underlying theme to guide what you do or don't do, or it might become something like a key statement or message. Maybe stick your piece of paper up under the stairs, so if things feel a bit much and you need a quick hide – and, who doesn't, sometimes? – it'll remind you of what's important.

Are you qualified?

Yes, you're qualified.

Easy.

This would be the shortest chapter in the world if we stopped here, but I guess you might not believe me. And fair enough, I struggled with this issue a lot myself, thinking there were surely people who were more qualified than me. Who was I to be giving it a bash?

Here's an awful and awe-full truth: many publicly elected positions don't require any formal qualification. There's no test. There's often no training either, after you get in. For many decision-making positions, if you can manage to get enough voters to vote for you, then you're in.

Whiiiich, explains quite a lot of things, if you think about it.

This isn't to say that learning about budgets, finance or even company law wouldn't help significantly in some roles. However, you can learn those things too, without doing an MBA.

When you think about it, being able to 'just get elected' might explain why we get egotists and sociopaths in many roles. People with normal-sized egos, who were raised to work hard but never put themselves forward, would find the thought of, and the process of, standing for election to be torture.

I did.

That's why I did a deal with myself to do it my way, without doing things that made me cringe. More on that later. We're talking about you right now.

I've got a good feeling about you.

➜ Structural inequality

Many decision-making roles are currently set up to suit people with a certain kind of education, who don't live with disability, and who have someone to look after most other aspects of their lives so they can concentrate on this single job.

The rules or customs of these roles are a structure – and if they stop some people from being represented, then you could say that these structures create inequality.

Do people stand to speak at meetings? Do they attend sessions at night-time or during office hours? Do some meetings go on and on until someone drops dead or they end, i.e. they don't have a formal finish time? Are reports lengthy and written in very formal English?

Who can't perform these roles because of the rules? Well, people who can't stand up, who work full-time or have caring responsibilities, or who can't read and digest information easily or at all when it's printed because of their vision or dyslexia or because English is just one of their languages.

If you're considering trying to be elected for a particular role, look at the buildings where your decision-makers meet. What do you notice? Is there an assumption that everyone will drive there in a car, or that you can afford parking if you do drive? Does everyone need to walk up stairs or down long hallways? If you couldn't hear, could you participate in the meeting? Do the toilets suit one group of people, while making others feel uncomfortable? Or do some people have to walk a long way to find safe, private toilets? Are there loos with grab bars, space to manoeuvre a mobility device and somewhere to change or feed a baby? Is there anywhere safe to leave children during meetings?

These are all things you could raise right now with people currently doing the job – they're the ones who could change the rules. Otherwise, try to get someone elected who'll try to change the rules. You can see the catch-22 there though, right? Only people who can work within the current structures can perform the role and try to make some changes.

Rules and customs and buildings themselves prevent some people from becoming decision-makers. It's nothing to do with their intelligence, drive or capability.

So, if there are structural challenges that make it difficult for you or others to get elected or do the job once elected, don't beat yourself up. You can only do so much in your life if there are real barriers. Perhaps you might find that it's worth mentioning these barriers in your campaign.

That being said, don't base your whole campaign on 'fighting the terrible system', since by standing for election you're trying to get a role within that system. Focus on positives: your voters will find it motivating and inspiring if you identify barriers, show examples of organisations who've benefited from their removal, and outline tangible, achievable steps that can be taken to change the current state of things.

Privacy and shame

Most of us have done things we'd prefer not to see on the front page of the paper (as those in the PR business used to say) or in internet searches.

That being said, I don't want you to let fear or shame stop you from standing for election. Accept that some things might come out about you – but they probably won't.

Talk to a trusted friend or counsellor if you want to rationalise whatever it is you're worried might be used against you. They can help you to think through how you might handle it becoming public.

My recommendation for responding to anything true that's made public about you is to make it a non-story by agreeing with it:

Say, 'Yes. Yes, I did that.'

If it's not something you're proud of, say that.

If it's something you regret, or you wouldn't do now, or you made reparations for, or you had treatment for, say that.

If it's something you shouldn't have to feel ashamed about – e.g. a normal human thing to do with bodies, sex or relationships – just acknowledge it. If someone you trusted shared something private without your consent, then say that. That makes them a terrible person, not you.

If what's been said about you is a lie, say, 'I didn't do/say that.'

And, if it's a lie but still something you don't believe people should be made to feel ashamed about, you might say, 'I didn't do that. Though, if I had <done that thing>, I don't think it's anything to be ashamed about.'

"Thank goodness you're here!"

This might not work for you, but I thought about the main thing that worried me and had a frank conversation with my brothers about it, in general terms. After a bit of a pause in the phone call, they acknowledged what I'd said and then changed the subject. It was awkward for a moment, but I knew they'd be prepared in the unlikely event a grumpy ex shared anything personal.

Gosh, that sounds like I've had a much more exciting past than I really have.

Early on, tell your family and friends that if any media people ring to talk about you, for any reason, to say 'No comment.' Easy. Send them directly to you. That's good common sense, particularly because they probably haven't thought about it and your Dad might tell stories about that time after you ate borscht when you were seven and the next morning you thought –

Anyway.

Please don't let fear or shame stop you from standing. I don't want all our decision-makers to be people who've lived their lives entirely shrink-wrapped and protected from mistakes and challenges. Or people who've done dastardly things but who are completely unabashed about it.

If something you're ashamed about does become public and you handle it with dignity, you'll find yourself some new fans who've also had lives with challenges. Most people are relieved to know that other people are open about the fact that they didn't have a home for a year, had problems with alcohol or other drugs for a while, got divorced or once lost their licence for speeding.

➡ Why you don't need to develop a thick skin and what you can do instead

People kept telling me I'd need to develop a thick skin if I was going into politics. I gathered they thought I was a bit soft or 'nice' and that only utter sociopaths could survive politics.

It's an understandable conclusion: a lot of the news we see about people in power suggests that politics is a dog-eat-dog game where everyone's trying to kick someone else before they get kicked. I don't agree with that. If we expect people to behave that way, then that's what we end up with.

Don't lose the ability to feel the things that make you human. Rather than developing a uniformly thick skin, learn to be selective about who affects you. I was, and still am, determined to remain warm-hearted, hard-headed and to develop the skills to have difficult conversations and deal with challenging things. I'm a relatively gentle person and that's OK.

Here's my best alternative to developing a thick skin (whatever that really means):

> **Decide whose opinions you care about. Pick a couple. Let them help you check your moral compass.**

In my case, there's a core group of people in my life I'd hate to let down. If they told me they were disappointed by something I'd said or done, I'd stop and have a good hard look at myself. Maybe I'd decide they didn't have all the information about why I did what I did, or I'd decide to do things differently next time. But I'd take their opinions on board.

Other than that, there are quite a few people who know me reasonably well. Their opinions would be interesting

"Thank goodness you're here!"

13

information and would be worth considering, but they wouldn't be show stoppers.

And everyone else? Well, if they don't truly know me, they can't judge me effectively one way or another.

Plan to do this alone

Make sure you can run your campaign yourself.

Obviously, if you're planning to run an enormous campaign and recruiting a manager and volunteers, this advice doesn't apply to you. However, for anyone who's trying to organise their own local campaign, I think it's easier to plan around doing it all yourself, and then, if you get willing and able helpers, doing things from your 'nice to have' list.

There's a good chance that a few people will jump on board to help with your campaign and go above and beyond because they really believe in what you're doing. But don't be surprised if the people you're expecting to pitch in will quietly absent themselves. That's an observation I've made about some people's creative and career-related projects. They expect their partners or families to enthusiastically jump in with support, then feel resentful when they don't. Other people have their own lives.

I've heard many authors – even hugely successful ones – say that their family and friends have never read their books. It doesn't mean they don't love or admire you. It might not be their thing.

Stand for election because you want to do it. Welcome any useful help along the way, while knowing you can cover all the basics yourself if required. Plan to do it the way that suits you. Be your own biggest supporter.

"Thank goodness you're here!"

Self-care

If you're an introvert, the idea of planning ways to ask people to vote for you might make you want to hide in the cupboard for a few months.

I found it useful to think of my election campaign as work or a project, rather than as selling or promoting myself. When I mentally separated the campaign from my feelings, it was easier to make decisions about what I needed to do.

Don't underestimate how stressful running a campaign can be. This might be the first time you've put yourself out for other people's judgement and really backed yourself. Good on you! But make sure you take care of your stress levels, stay in touch with level-headed people who know you and care about you, and try to create a bit of distance between your campaign and your self-worth.

➡ **Make it fun however you can**

You can make this whole campaigning thing a lot more manageable and, dare I say, fun with a few tricks. Maybe fun is too big a call. But I enjoyed building in some energy boosters, jokes with myself and stress relievers wherever possible.

Have you thought about making yourself a personal soundtrack to your campaign? You know how some movies have really stirring, empowering music throughout? You can make that for yourself. Why not make your election an epic adventure with a soundtrack to match? Create a walk-on track to pep you up before you do something challenging. Walk-on music is what comedians use to create energy as they walk on stage. It gets them and the crowd into the mood.

Some people find it reassuring to have a talisman: a favourite item of clothing, keyring, lucky shoes, jewellery, cologne or colour that makes them feel solid and like themselves.

"Thank goodness you're here!"

Why not wear something distinctive that you get a kick out of?

Then it'll serve two purposes – it'll make you feel good and it can make you recognisable. That sparkly brooch or tam-o'-shanter or leopard print coat could become your 'thing'.

Other ideas for making your campaign fun:

- Ride your bike everywhere.

- Invite different friends to come to various events, so you get to spend time with them and they see what you're doing.

- Reward yourself when you do things that you find challenging.

- Take photos everywhere you go, so you're stopping and enjoying the world around you while creating a creative stockpile you might use for your campaign posts.

- Give yourself a challenge of making a certain number of new contacts every time you go somewhere.

- Visit every coffee shop in your suburb or town.

I'm sure your ideas and mine differ when it comes to fun, but you get the idea. Work out what you'll find motivating so you can plug away at your campaign plan without getting burned out.

"Thank goodness you're here!"

Being memorable

Anything that makes you memorable is an advantage. People have extremely short attention spans and tend to 'file' information in their brains in small chunks. They might remember you as the tall footballer, or the red-haired accountant or the white-haired person with the bike.

Some people get a lot of free kicks because they're in a profession that's universally respected as full of smart people: lawyers, doctors, teachers … If an accountant stands for local city council, most people will think, 'Oh good, we need someone who understands money.' They won't check if the person almost failed all their Uni courses and now works for crime lords. If you're lucky enough to work in a respected profession, milk it for all it's worth.

Names are important. You definitely need people to remember your name. Do you have a famous name? For example, some politicians have family names that go back for generations and they're memorable.

Take a look at how your name will appear on the voting papers – if it'll appear with the surname in all capitals and in bold, then write it that way on all your campaign materials.

You might want to run under your nickname, if it's memorable or easier to say than your real name, so long as it'll be the name people will see on the voting papers.

If your name isn't memorable or scintillating, is there something about you that people remark on when you meet them? Something physical? Do you have silver hair, big shoulders or stunning tattoos? Something about your work or hobbies? Are you a teacher, plumber or blues singer? Something about your dress sense? Do you wear sharp jackets, a lot of yellow or cat brooches made from real cat hair you felted from your cat, Mr Tigglepaws?

If you're a rock-climbing librarian, people will find that memorable.

If none of these rings bells, don't panic. You're totally cool. I'm picking off the super-easy and obvious first things many people don't

"Thank goodness you're here!"

realise they can use to their advantage. Ask your friends how they'd describe you if they were trying to talk you up. You might sound more interesting than you'd thought.

Your appearance

Elections are a lot like auditions or job interviews. At the end of the campaign, voters choose the people who seem like they could do the role. Often the only thing they'll have to go on is your appearance in photos, seeing you speak at an event or maybe seeing things you write.

When someone doesn't know you, they'll be asking themselves: 'Does this person look like they could do the job?' So your appearance needs to say:

- I understand what this job is about.

- I'm ready and able to do this job.

- I wouldn't embarrass you if I was representing your group/city/whatever.

You'll get advice from well-meaning people who say, 'Don't worry about it, just be yourself!' and 'We should allow people to dress however they want.'

Sure. Heaps of things 'should' be different. However, the reality is, if you want to get your bum on a seat in a place where you can make some changes, you might need to modify your style to demonstrate to people that you know the 'rules' of that place and you can do the job.

When I say rules, I don't mean written-down rules, I mean the things that most people do or wear in a particular social setting.

As for 'just be yourself'… let's say that I generally feel most myself dressed as a pirate while drinking pina coladas and dancing to the Scissor Sisters. I still don't choose to do that everywhere I go. It's not appropriate and it doesn't show good judgement.

"Thank goodness you're here!"

One way I show good judgement in social situations is by dressing to suit the occasion. This demonstrates that I know the 'rules' of these occasions. If I don't know what's appropriate, I ask around or do some research about what's the done thing.

I'm still myself when I go to a funeral, show up at court or go out with friends, but I dress differently for those things. I express my own personal style in those situations, but I modify my appearance to be respectful of others by not making the funeral all about me, to avoid going to jail, or to get the attention of that hot bartender.

Voters will be looking for clues about what you're really like. If you dress in a way that seems like you don't know what's going on around you or you don't follow accepted social rules, you'll come off as unobservant or inconsiderate, or a deliberate rule-breaker. And who wants an unobservant, inconsiderate rule-breaker making rules for their community?

Context is essential.

Imagine the same person wearing a very expensive suit, with slicked back hair, on the following candidate posters:

Vote 1 Baxter Baxwell
Smith St Tree-climbing Club

Vote 1 Baxter Baxwell
State Senate

Vote 1 Baxter Baxwell
Mechanics Union representative

I talk a lot more about appearance in Chapter 4: What to wear.

➡ **When you don't fit the norm, use their uniform to your advantage**

Some people have to work harder than others to prove that they're worthy, that the way they think and what they have to say is valuable. It's not a level playing field. If you look different or come from a different background to the other people who are assumed to be a good fit, then you're up against it.

Let's say you're standing for election and most of the people who've done the job in the past have been older, male bankers or lawyers from a particular cultural or religious background. If your skin colour is different to theirs, or you use a wheelchair or other mobility aids when they don't, or you don't present as stereotypically male, then you obviously look different from them.

What can you do? Work out what their 'uniform' or 'rules' are and adapt them to suit yourself.

If they're all in suits and ties, then do the same, but with your own style. Wear a tailored, fuchsia-coloured suit jacket or a sober suit with a brightly printed tie. Wear business-wear and use striking-coloured mobility aids. Get a suit jacket tailored to look good if you're sometimes or always seated in a rollator or wheelchair. You might create your own uniform of a well-cut t-shirt under a blazer.

Make a nod to the rules to show that you understand the uniform and that you understand the role you're keen to take on. If you look different, you can't and shouldn't need to hide that. Use visual cues to demonstrate that you understand and are capable of doing the job – and you're going to do it your way.

Chapter 2

Thinking this through

"Thank goodness you're here!"

How would your life change if you got elected?

It's worth thinking about what life might be like if you get the job, by which I mean get elected. I don't want to put you off, but I do want you to have a serious think about these things as you read this book.

Time: Will your current employer give you time off to run your campaign? If elected, can you continue to do your current work? How long is the term for this role? Do you know how often you'd need to attend meetings? How much time would you need to devote to preparing for those meetings? What else would you be expected to do – answer calls and emails and attend events and write speeches and talk to the press …?

Personal organisation: Would you have to make sure you always have a change of clothes with you in case of last-minute events or meetings? Would you need to look presentable every time you left the house? Is it possible people might expect you to have all kinds of facts and figures at your fingertips at all hours of the day and night?

Your career and interests: How will you make sure your work, important relationships and your own hobbies and interests will get enough time in your schedule? Is this role a good fit for your personality, your skills and talents?

Relationships and responsibilities: Would you need to arrange for carers at short notice? How might your partner or partners feel about sharing you every time you're in public, if you have the kind of role or profile that makes people feel like they know you and can talk to you at length about whatever's on their mind.

Money: Will you lose work, income or opportunities by doing this? Does the role pay a stipend or other kind of salary? Maybe you'll end up financially better off. If you receive income or perks from this position, will this affect your income tax?

"Thank goodness you're here!"

22

Your sense of self: How will you feel about having to keep a lot of things confidential? Not being able to share things with your friends or family, not being able to make flippant off-hand remarks in case they're misinterpreted, not being able to be silly …

I found all those things pretty hard because I like a laugh.

It's worth talking about all these considerations with a counsellor or logical friend, so you can weigh up the decision to stand for this role, or whether there are other ways you can contribute to the kinds of decisions that are made in your community.

Find a mentor or a supportive organisation

You can learn a lot from people who've been there before you, and who might have considerable energy to lend to your campaign.

Ask around.

It's very likely that you'll find a group of like-minded people who support the things you're wanting to do. These might be groups who share your interests, or they might be specifically set up to get particular kinds of people elected. Most major political parties offer support to prospective candidates; however, there are also non-politically aligned groups to encourage people to stand for elections.

I found a local government women's group (ALGWA) after I saw an ad about sessions to encourage women into local government. Most of the members were former or current councillors from all around the state where I live. They also found me an amazing mentor who'd done the role I was trying to get elected to do. Not only was she clever and funny, she shared some incredibly useful information with me.

The people who spend their time helping other people to get elected to decision-making roles are often the kinds of nice people you hope exist in the world. So, just being around them can be a balm to

"Thank goodness you're here!"

your spirit if you're starting to feel cynical about decision-makers and politics.

They've seen it all and often have very canny ways of dealing with racism, sexism, bad behaviour, back-stabbing and machinations in all kinds of organisations.

If you get help through an organisation, consider joining as an official member. Groups need members to keep on helping people. For what is usually a tiny joining fee, you'll bolster something that's been important to you and will be important to others. And look, don't just join, consider being an active member and perhaps even getting onto their board or committee. It's another kind of decision-making role where your skills could be really valuable.

Yes, joining groups and taking part in their activities takes time. Since you've read this far, I'm betting you're the type who makes time and probably gets a lot done.

If you find a group of people you like, doing things you think are important, I reckon that spending time with them could make your life feel rich and worthwhile. It could lead you in a new direction, regardless of how you go with your campaign.

A mentor is incredibly valuable. It might be hard to believe that someone will give up so much of their personal time to answer your questions and attend meetings with you and give you information, but these people exist.

If someone mentors you, make sure you thank them well and often and see whether you can somehow contribute to their work or life. At the very least, promise yourself that you'll give at least this much effort to someone else during your life.

"Thank goodness you're here!"

Money matters

Can you afford this?

If you're standing for a federal election, that's going to require a different kind of commitment than if you're joining the advisory committee for your local guinea pig-appreciation society.

But for many types of campaigns, if you focus on ways to get in touch with your required number of voters, you might discover it'll take time and creativity more than it does money. Focus is your friend when it comes to your campaign budget. When you focus on the people you want to spend time with and talk with, you can work out how much it might cost to reach them. I'll talk about this in detail in Chapter 3: Your people.

You can either fit your campaign tasks to the money you have available, or you can work out what you want to do and the cost, then look at how much you have and start fundraising to make up the difference.

Your perspective – and approach – may depend on whether you're campaigning for a role that will pay, or for one that will cost you time and even reduce your income. Your anticipated monetary rewards might give you a different idea about what's a reasonable amount of money to dedicate to your campaign.

Some people think budgets are boring, but most of us are extremely creative when we're given constraints. Think of your budget as your creativity super-booster.

So, how much will you spend on your campaign?

Apart from money you think you might spend, factor in any lost earnings from time you'll spend on your campaign, rather than doing jobs as a self-employed or casual worker.

I allowed a budget of A$2,000. I also spent a year planning and running my local government campaign, so I lost about half my normal income from my consultancy for that year. I planned to do all

"Thank goodness you're here!"

my own graphic design and communications, since I had the skills and a kind designer friend who offered to help me if I got stuck.

Setting a budget helps you avoid the last-minute temptations and pressures when one of the other candidates buys a hot air balloon in the shape of their head or sign-writes a fleet of sausage dogs.

And, as I've mentioned previously in this chapter, can you afford to do the role if you get elected to do it?

Why are you doing this again? Find your scrap of paper from the exercise you did in the Why you? section and remind yourself.

It's likely you're standing for election because you think you'll have more influence as a decision-maker who's inside the 'tent' than outside it. No matter what happens, after running a campaign you'll be more confident and assured, you'll have developed a perfect Goldilocks (just-right) handshake or elbow bump, plus you'll have stories for your novel that you could never have made up.

Oh, the stories.

But let's not get sidetracked.

Asking for money can turn out to be a nice thing to do

After a bit of a delay, I invited people to donate to my campaign.

It made me feel sick, because I was raised to help others and never ask for help, especially financial help. However, I put a button on my website linked to PayPal and when people asked how they could contribute, I said I was looking for help and donations to help me reach 1,337 people. That was 'my number': the number of number 1 votes I estimated that I needed to get elected. (If you want to know how to work out your number, check out Chapter 3: What's your number?)

You know what? Some people will be immensely grateful to give you money rather than being asked to go doorknocking. Or they might want to help but don't have skills you'd need, so are happy to flick you some dosh. For some people, giving you fifty or a couple of hundred dollars or even more is easy for them.

By the way, speaking of doorknocking, I didn't do any.

I've done a fair bit of it to support other people's state or federal campaigns, so my decision was based on a time-and-motion assessment rather than a dislike of doorknocking. For more on this subject, see Chapter 5: Doorknocking and why you might not need to do it.

Be really specific about what donated money will help you to do, e.g.

$20 will buy 3 posters
$40 will buy 50 car stickers
$50 will buy 600 notecards

Here in Australia, money you make through donations can count as taxable income, so check the tax rules where you live and record that money on your spreadsheet as well.

All of your donors will be investing in you. They're your true believers. Give them love. Contact them regularly, just to tell them what's going on and how you're feeling. It's such a boost to keep talking to people who support what you're doing. Don't forget to also give them your campaign materials to pass along to their friends.

I was given A$1,426 of donations. The act of asking and receiving this support was more valuable than the dollars themselves. I felt like other people were backing me – they wanted me to do this. It took the campaign from an idea inside my head, out into the world.

➡ **A note about money – know the rules**

The financial side of your campaign could cause you problems if you don't know the rules about what you can spend and the implications of receiving donations.

- You might be able to claim the costs of campaigning in your next tax return.

- Your election might limit the amount of money you're allowed to spend on different kinds of things and require you to put in a statement at the end of your campaign.

"Thank goodness you're here!"

27

- Donations you receive could count as income and affect your next tax return.

Work out the rules and limits and set up a simple spreadsheet to track the things you need to account for.

Talk to your accountant or check your tax department's website to find out what happens to any money you receive as donations.

You'll look like a wally if you win the election then are sacked because you didn't follow the spending rules.

Know the election deadlines

Got someone who's willing to help you, who loves organising information? If they are also a stationery geek, this is just the task for them.

Get them to look up all the election deadlines and put them onto a calendar for you. Electronic or hard copy: this is essential.

You might find it motivating to write the campaign key dates on a big wall planner. Once you can see what needs to be done by when, you can work back from there. It might help you stick to your priorities.

Imagine campaigning merrily away and then realising you're not really a candidate because you forgot to put in your nomination.

If you're standing for a government election, look up the electoral rules in your area. Australia has electoral commissions who are tasked with advertising, running and managing local, state and federal elections. They're usually more than happy to answer questions or point you to useful information. They often hold information sessions for upcoming elections.

They're also staffed by people who vote, so be pleasant in all your dealings with them.

Know the election rules

Figuring out the rules up front lets you get organised and avoid wasting your time.

You should be able to get the rules governing your kind of election from the organisation you're trying to join, or from the groups who manage the election. There's no way around downloading them all, reading through, highlighter pencil in hand, tongue poking out the corner of your mouth, if that's what helps you think most clearly, and making notes. Put anything time-related onto your campaign calendar, with reminders ahead of time to make sure you meet the critical deadlines.

get a handy template

Are you eligible to stand in your area? That's the most important question. If you're not eligible, then stop right now.

For some types of elections you might have to be a resident, or a member of the organisation you're wanting to be elected to, or have been a member for a particular period.

Rules vary considerably from place to place, and for government elections you will sometimes have to keep to both federal and local government rules. Where I live it's the local governments who decide when signs go up and come down, but the federal government decides that they must have certain information on them, such as the authorising person and their address and the name and address of the printer.

How many yard signs can you have? Do your flyers have to be authorised by someone and have the name and address of the printer on them? How big can your signs be? When can signs be put up and when must they come down?

There really can be a lot of rules. Enlist a nerdy, rule-following friend who's happy to help you to work them all out. Promise they won't have to do any doorknocking and they'll be sweet.

"Thank goodness you're here!"

Ignore everyone

Yes. Ignore everyone.

Ignore me if you want. I'm offering my thoughts from where I stand – there are a lot of other perspectives.

You'll find that everyone you know suddenly becomes a freaking expert on election campaigns. But, not to be too harsh about it, most of the people who will give you advice don't know what they're talking about. And they're also unlikely to be jumping in to help with yours.

Do some research on campaigning, prepare to run your entire campaign yourself and invite advice-givers to help (they'll usually consider their advice to be a tremendous gift and otherwise decline to help) and just say, 'Thanks,' and then ignore it.

Unless it's really funny, in which case write it down for your memoir.

The really helpful people will ask what you're planning to do and ask how they can help. They might have expertise in particular areas but they'll still ask first, rather than launching into advice-delivery mode.

Advice-givers can freak you out and make you doubt yourself. Keep a notebook of campaign ideas. Write down the things you definitely won't do, as reassurance and so you don't waste time reconsidering them. Your notebook could live inside a note-taking app or it could be a real book. Use something you'll always have with you. If you're a people-pleaser, write down everyone's advice into the back of the book, then they'll feel happy that you've captured their solid gold suggestion and you can go through it later to see whether it's useful.

Ignoring everyone is very liberating. It may become very important in your life.

OK. Don't ignore absolutely everyone.

Identify the outstanding cheer squad of people you respect and whose respect you value, who will tell you if you're being a silly sausage, and check in with them sometimes. Listen to them, but still, don't let them get you completely off track.

Build a database

I put a lot of effort into meeting as many nice people as possible and getting their essential contact details. Everything in my campaign plan relied on having laid the groundwork by collecting the right information for the final phase. At voting time, this involved contacting everyone on my list and asking them to contact their contacts to ask them to vote for me. I believe this final effort helped me reach a significant number of usually-non-voting potential voters.

Be aware before you get stuck into your campaign that you are absolutely going to need a great contact list, arranged in a way that's easy to manage and add to as you go. I cover this in detail in Chapter 4: Getting your stuff together.

get a handy template

"Thank goodness you're here!"

Chapter 3

Your people

Who? Never heard of them!

Your aim isn't to make sure NO-ONE says that when they read your name – your aim is to make sure that ENOUGH people DO know your name. And then vote for it. For you. You know what I mean.

What's your number?

If you can work out the number of votes you need, you'll know how and where to spend your time and energy.

If you're standing for a student representative council, you'll know how many students are at your school. They're all potential voters. However, if you find out that typically only 25% of students vote, then this gives you more information.

How many positions are being filled in the election?

How many other people do you think will be standing for election?

Statistics can be really useful to help you work out how to plan your campaign. See what you can find out about previous elections.

It's worth figuring out how your voting system works too, so you can tell your likely voters what to do. Otherwise they might waste their vote if they misunderstand how it all works.

➡ **How I worked out my number and what else the statistics told me**

I got a nerdy friend to look at how the voting system worked for my election, and we decided that 1,337 was 'my number' – the number of people I needed to vote for me and give me their number 1 preference (as they'd vote 1, 2, 3 etc for the people they wanted elected). 1,337 was the quota of required votes from a previous election.

We used statistics about past elections to work out the average number of candidates, the total number of voters and the age groups of the people who tended to vote. This was all vital information because it told me that people in my age group tended not to vote. Oh no! They were the ones I thought would share my values, and who I thought I could most easily reach.

I decided to concentrate a significant part of my campaign on making 'my people' aware of the election and how it affected them, then letting them know how few people voted and effectively chose the elected reps.

This may make you glaze over, but here goes. In Tasmania (my home state in Australia) local council elections use the Hare-Clark proportional voting system. A candidate may romp it in, being elected with lots of votes. Once they pass the required quota, all their voting slips are re-examined and whoever their voters wrote down as their #2 choice gets these votes (at a reduced proportion) added to their votes until they also reach the quota and are elected. At this point, their votes are also redistributed, so there's a trickle-down effect. And there's also a trickle-up effect (this is not the way the local electoral commission describes things, but I'm giving you my summary) whereby the unfortunate person who receives the smallest number of votes is excluded. All of their votes get distributed to whoever was given #2 votes on their voting slips.

There's value in being not-the-most unpopular within this system. Spoiler: I was elected with only 704 #1 votes and enough trickle-down or trickle-up votes to receive the fourth highest number of first preference votes in that election. Considering there were 12 incumbents (people who'd already been doing the role who were standing for re-election), it was pretty good to get this kind of result as someone without a public profile.

Knowing how this voting system worked meant I could tell people who said they'd already decided who they were voting for that I'd be happy with their #2, #3 or #4 votes. I knew those would all add up for me if I wasn't excluded early. And they did.

"Thank goodness you're here!"

Who are your people?

Now you've got some idea of your number (the number of votes you think you'll need to get elected) you can focus on finding the people who'll vote for you.

If you found statistics about previous elections, you might have found general info about who voted – their age groups, for instance, or areas in which they live. You might look at popular candidates and see if you can work out what kinds of people liked them and why.

People you know

The most obvious, and least stressful, place to start is with people you already know. Use your contacts list, database or spreadsheet to sort these into people who are eligible to vote for you and those who aren't. Don't write off people who aren't eligible to vote but who have good networks. I had several tabs on my spreadsheet: strong supporters, likely supporters, people I was unsure about and people to avoid.

Now's a great time to get in touch with the people you think will be strong supporters, tell them you're thinking of standing for election and give them the important info, like the election date. Ask them for permission to add their details to your contact database. And confirm whether you've got their up-to-date email, phone number and postal address.

If you're already up and running with your campaign, now's the time to start inviting people out for coffee or drinks.

By talking to your close contacts now, you'll get some positive energy, offers of support and some hot tips.

Aim to get the contact details for every encouraging person you talk to about your campaign. Learn to say, 'Can I add you to my mailing list? I'd like to invite you to some events' and 'I'd love your vote.'

get a handy template

"Thank goodness you're here!"

Working out what might prevent 'your' people from voting for you

Think about all the reasons 'your people' might not actually get around to voting for you, then work out how to sort these challenges out.

In Chapter 7: Challenges there's a list of all the blockers I thought might prevent otherwise-supportive people from voting for me. You might need to address specific issues at different phases of your campaign.

Common blockers are that 'your people':

- are not registered to vote
- were once registered but have been dropped off the rolls
- feel cynical about politics and don't realise how their vote affects anything
- have never met a fabulous person like you who wants to do this kind of role
- don't know anything about the role that you're trying to get elected to
- don't know when the election is, or how and where to vote
- can't get to the voting place
- find it overwhelming to choose between candidates
- forget to vote, despite their good intentions
- think all politicians or people wanting to be decision-makers are corrupt.

Reaching your people

Your main goal in your election campaign, if you want me to boil it down for you, is to be likeable, look credible and be memorable.

Likeable people are ones who:

- make eye contact

- smile

- remember our name

- ask us questions

- seem similar to us – things that we think are important seem to be important to them too

- seem to have reasonable self-control and judgement – they dress and behave appropriately for events, they don't blab or badmouth people.

I talked about looking credible in Chapter 1: Your appearance, but to summarise: people will look at you and ask themselves, 'Do they look like someone who could do this role?'.

Being memorable involves giving people reasons to remember your name and something about you, so they recognise you on the voting form and have things to tell their friends about you.

Get a recommendation from someone you trust, who's connected

If you're recommended by a well-respected person, that's a massive benefit.

The easiest and most comfortable way to meet people is to ask people you know if they'll introduce you to their friends. You might feel a bit weird asking this, but it's way less cringey than trying to approach strangers.

Find people who like you and who talk to lots of other people. My bet is that beauticians, hairdressers, taxi drivers, newsagents, bottle-shop workers, bartenders and butchers might be the biggest

"Thank goodness you're here!"

influencers in your town. If you're a vegetarian, get to know your local wholefoods store staff. Find a café you like and become a regular. Make them your most-visited people. Ask their opinion on your campaign ideas. People love to give opinions and feel like trusted advisers. They often know good places to put up posters or leave flyers – they might even offer to let you leave them at their premises. And when their other customers start talking to them about the election, guess who they'll talk about?

Close, personal communication is most effective

What are the most persuasive methods of communication? In my experience, they're the ones that are most personal.

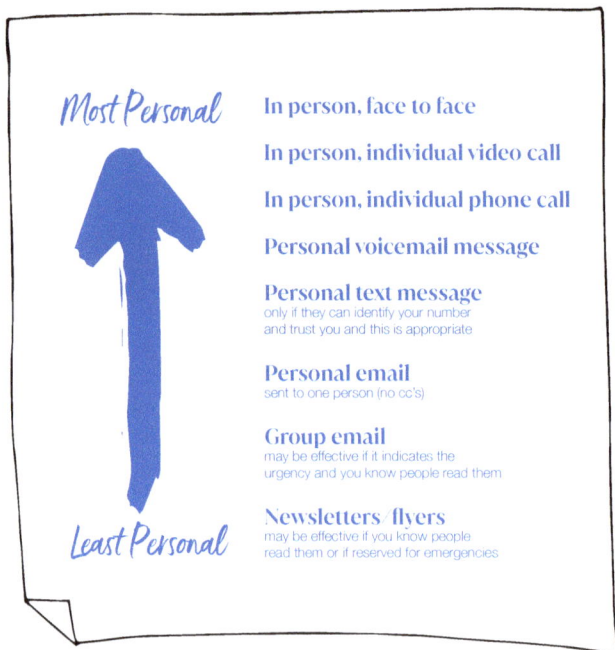

Most Personal

In person, face to face

In person, individual video call

In person, individual phone call

Personal voicemail message

Personal text message
only if they can identify your number and trust you and this is appropriate

Personal email
sent to one person (no cc's)

Group email
may be effective if it indicates the urgency and you know people read them

Newsletters/flyers
may be effective if you know people read them or if reserved for emergencies

Least Personal

If you can, meet people in person. That's your strongest and most personal way of forming a connection.

These are what I consider the most-effective through to least-effective ways of getting someone to know and care about you enough to vote:

- Face to face
- Phone call or video call
- Personal letter
- Personal email
- Personal text message
- Direct Message conversation on social media
- Speaking to a group
- Social media personal mention or comment
- Email newsletter written so it seems personal
- Social media post
- Social media video
- Leaflets or flyers
- Posters and signs
- Newspaper advertising

You might order this list differently, but still, try to make as many of your contacts as personal as possible. It's tempting to get desperate and kid yourself that shaking a wobble board with your name on it by the side of the highway is helping you to reach thousands of commuters; however, most of them will think you're selling pizza and the rest might think uncharitable thoughts about you.

Think about it – what makes you feel valued by someone you've met? A group email or a text that starts out asking how your cat's operation went?

"Thank goodness you're here!"

What makes you want to get to know someone more? A shouty VOTE FOR JOHN TRY-HARD-SMITH flyer in your letterbox or an invitation to a community discussion on a subject you care about?

If you're doing the type of election campaign that relies on you getting your name in front of thousands of strangers, then of course you can't personally meet them all. But, if you start out by prioritising the most personal methods, and return to these whenever possible, you'll make great authentic relationships and people will be more willing to talk about you (in a good way) to all the people they know. Focus on quality.

➡ **Tips for making connections**

Shaking a hand, touching an elbow, handing something to someone, taking a coat to hang it – these are all ways to create a connection without being creepy. Human beings can respond well to non-creepy touch. Researchers have researched this. Use your judgement. As for most things, when it comes to touching someone, if in doubt, don't.

Strike up conversations with neutral topics so you can gently get the ball rolling with strangers. Is that a new smart watch you're wearing? Are you standing in the queue? I don't want to push in, hahahah. Do you know how long this café is open until? I didn't check the weather forecast this morning: do you know what this afternoon is going to be like? I like your bike – where's a safe place to lock up a bike near Main Road? Oh, your labraspoodle seems to have an upset tummy – I'll grab you some more plastic bags and possibly a trowel.

Finding new people who share your interests or values

There are quite a few ways to meet people in person. The nicest and most authentic way is to find people who do things you're genuinely interested in, rather than inserting yourself everywhere and faking nice. If you spend your campaign going to places you like with people you like, your life and your campaign will feel enjoyable.

Do you belong to any clubs or groups? How many people belong to those clubs? How many people do you know personally?

What sorts of places or events do you love going to? What sorts of topics do you enjoy talking about? What sorts of books do you read? These are all clues to the kinds of groups of people you should prioritise and topics you might talk about during your campaign.

People trust organisations they're a part of. So, consider joining or being more active in organisations that do things you care about. Don't join everything, obviously. But do sign up to newsletters for interesting groups, follow their social media accounts, comment on and share their posts and attend their events. If they do put out a newsletter, consider advertising in it or asking if you can contribute an article.

Note: if what you're writing counts as an election ad, triple-check to make sure you're not infringing the rules about when you can advertise and what needs to be written in your advertisements.

Do they have meetings? Can you go along? Talk to the president beforehand, preferably before the day of the meeting, to say that you're standing for election and coming along to hear what's important to the group. They might introduce you. They might also tell you to nick off, but that's unlikely. They'll probably be flattered that you're interested in their group and keen to size you up. Offer to speak at their events or to be an interviewer or MC if they need one.

Make it clear you're not coming to do a hard sell – just to listen. That being said, have all of your flyers or business cards or promotional rock candy with tiny pictures of your smiling face in the centre ready to give to people.

Ask if they'd consider hosting a candidate's forum nearer to the election. You'd be surprised by how many community groups are interested in doing this to have a look at the candidates up close.

Anything that will get you in front of a group of like-minded people is a plus, even if it makes your guts churn. Getting your opponents in there next to you at a candidates' forum, especially if they're not a good fit for a particular group who'll like you best, will make you look and feel even better.

"Thank goodness you're here!"

Let them see or hear you or read what you've written

You can't meet everyone. If you want to reach larger numbers of people, you might consider speaking on a panel, on TV, radio, podcast or a video on social media. You can also write for papers or sites that'll be widely read.

I get right into this in Chapter 5: Campaigning nitty gritty.

As with anything you do with your precious time and election budget, only do things your target voters will see and enjoy. Otherwise, skip it.

You'll doubtless have people advising you to get on the latest 'young people's' platform. But, let's face it, even if the young-'uns are having an ace time watching each other Tok-Takking or Yik-Yakking or DanceFacing, the last thing in the world they want to see is someone the advanced age of their Aunty Jess on there in her fun blazer saying, 'Hey, you crazy kids! Let's talk about voting while I do a totally sick dance!'

A 'young person' just told me that no-one makes obviously edited videos any more. (They also missed the irony in my use of the words 'ace' and 'totally sick'.) Videos should look like you shot them yourself using your phone because you had a thought you wanted to share with your dear watcher while strolling on a mountain trail. In the same way carelessly 'undone' hairstyles take a lot of effort to create, easy breezy handheld videos are edited, so you'll need to learn how to do that. It can absorb a lot of time. If you like doing it and it comes easily and you can imagine your potential voters finding and watching it, then it's worth a shot, as people can get a sense of you as a person. And you'll get to visit mountain trails.

Give people something to hold and keep

While I'm not a fan of handing out impersonal campaign flyers that shout 'Vote 1 ME!', I do think there's value in giving people something keep-able when you talk to them. I talk about this more in Chapter 4: Working out what you need.

If you offer people something attractive and informative, that's aimed at the things they care about, then they're likely to keep it. Holding something you've given them can make a person feel that they have a piece of you – you're connected. If it's something they can pass along, then even better.

→ What about stalkers and haters?

It's natural to be worried about attracting stalkers, weirdos and trolls simply because you're standing for election. That's a real fear if you're sticking your head above the ramparts any time in life.

Happily, I didn't have any stalkers during my campaign. I didn't indulge the couple of grumpy people who tried to get a rise out of me on social media. I did attract a couple of harmless weirdos.

Think about whether you want to use your own phone number or get a new number you'll use for your campaign and, hopefully, after you're elected.

I used my personal mobile phone number throughout my campaign and received very few calls. I already work as a communications consultant with my number on my public website, so it seemed silly to try to keep it private when anyone could find it with a few clicks.

Some kinds of elections will require you to use a real address where you could reasonably expect to be found. That could be your work address – it might not need to be your home address. Check the rules for your election.

Be prepared to report any worrying behaviour directly to the police and to record anything that bothers you. No, you don't need the kind of thick skin that involves putting up with any abuse in any form.

"Thank goodness you're here?"

Chapter 4

Getting your stuff together

"Thank goodness you're here!"

What's your point? Messages, policies or platform

Overall, what's the thing you want someone to know, feel or do after they hear from you? That's your message. See Chapter 7: Anatomy of my campaign for the messages I developed for different parts of my campaign.

What do you want people to know, feel or do after hearing your messages?

- What do you care about?

- Why are you standing for election?

- What kind of person are you? What are your deep-seated values? How do you see the world?

- What do you like about the organisation you're hoping to be elected to join?

- What can you offer that organisation or the people voting for you?

- What do you hope to improve by being there?

I reckon it's better to come up with positive statements rather than talking about things you don't like, or complaining about people being corrupt or making poor decisions. That kind of talk tends to make your audience switch off. And, if you say everyone who's currently in those roles is bad, then the fact that you want to join them makes you seem a bit dubious too.

Think about how you can show people what's important to you, rather than telling them.

What do I mean?

Well, rather than saying 'I think early childhood education is important,' create links to events you go to that celebrate early childhood educators, or articles about the importance of quality teaching for young children, or photos of schoolbags and some

"Thank goodness you're here!"

45

statistics about all the things that improve in a child's life when they can attend engaging pre-school classes.

Look for links and articles and events and add these to a list of potential topics for blog posts or social media posts or events you can attend and invite others to.

How to write like a human being

There's something about writing for The Public that can make you pucker every puckerable part of your body.

Most of your competitors will be using the most turgid, uptight language possible. They'll all sound the same.

You, though? You're an interesting human being other human people will want to get to know.

One way to write like a human being is to imagine you're talking to a stranger at a bus stop. How would you explain the things you're interested in? Write down what you might say to them before the bus arrives. You'll probably use fairly short, everyday words. They're good.

Another thing you can do is to record yourself talking about your messages or the reasons why you're standing for election. Use your phone's recording function. Ignore how your voice sounds and listen to the words you use.

Or, next time you're talking to a friend about your campaign, ask them to repeat back to you what they think you said. Or listen when other people introduce you (if they do a good introduction). How do they describe what you're doing or what's important to you? Write down their phrases.

Whenever you write anything, ask yourself if you'd really speak that way to someone.

Remember that everything you write is a conversation with one person – only one person is reading your words at a time. Ask them questions. Don't be afraid to be irreverent. People love real humans. They're suspicious of buttoned-up, super-correct people who say whilst or amongst. Show your humanity and foibles and let them in on your hobbies and interests.

People will probably ask what you stand for or about your platform or your policies when you tell them you're standing for election. You might not have any actual policies if you're standing for a decision-making role that covers a large range of topics. I think what people are really asking with this question is, 'who are you' or 'what do you care about?' They're looking for clues that you care about similar things to them, that you're trustworthy and sane, that you'll be there to help in ways they think are useful.

Maybe they just want to know how you make decisions, more than they want to know about any specific subject. You'll tie yourself in knots trying to come up with an answer that suits everyone.

So, don't try to suit everyone.

And don't bother with coming up with an elevator pitch that'll delight everyone. It's easy to get sucked into trying to come up with a slogan or a catchy phrase, but you're not selling washing machines.

Whenever you're talking to someone, focus on the kinds of things you guess might interest them.

I had different messages for different types of people. I wasn't lying – I would just choose to talk about the thing they wanted to talk about. No point having a conversation they weren't interested in.

Making a plan

Does a plan sound crushingly boring? Maybe it gives you a little thrill. I use the term 'a plan' to mean: work out a way that you'll be able to remember and do all the essential parts of your election campaign by yourself.

get a handy template

Your plan needs to do a couple of things:

- remind you of the dates when important things need to happen, and what you'll need to do to prepare for those dates/things

- remind you of the messages you want to get across and who you want to get them across to (refer to the previous section) and make sure you schedule these over your campaign period.

Some people like to use computer spreadsheets or project planning software. You might prefer to draw yours and put it on a wall or keep it in your diary. I created a new Google calendar with all the key dates on it, so I could see both my regular calendar and my campaign calendar, with campaign things in a different colour.

You might like to use a physical calendar to record all the key dates and tasks, and a pad and paper as a to-do list.

Use whatever organisational tool has worked for you in the past when you've had to get something done by a particular date. Don't forget to factor in the lead times for different parts of your campaign. Do you need to print something? How much time do the printers need? How long will it take to organise events like your launch?

Work out your campaign schedule based on how much time you have available to do the most essential things, and add in other things where they might help you to reach more people who are likely to vote for you. Not just anyone, but the right kinds of people.

Highlight things you'd like to do if you had help, but otherwise schedule in the things you can do yourself.

If you find a marvellous, reliable person who's a wonderful organiser, who puts their hand up to help (and actually commits), give them some specific tasks. They might help you to make and keep track of your plan, or take charge of maintaining your mailing list and how many times you contact everyone, or find events you could attend, or perhaps even organise some events. Whatever they do for you, make sure you understand how it all works, in case you need to pick up where they leave off.

Working out what you need

You need:

- Photos – at minimum, a good headshot that you can use with your candidate statement or other promotional material. I talk about this in more detail in the next section.

- Messages – the things you want to say and ideas for how and when you want to say them.

- An email address that looks suitable for the type of election you are contesting – it may be circumspect not to use your teenage 'AngstyUnicorn779@hotmail.com' address.

- Phone number – you've got a few options. You can use your own. That's what I did because it's my work phone number and already on my business website, so it isn't private. Some people opt to get a new number.

  - You can get mobile phones that take two SIM cards, so you could have your own private number on one SIM card and your new/professional/burner number for your campaign on another SIM card and receive and make all calls using the same phone.

  - You could pay for a 1300 number (in Australia – your country likely has something similar) that diverts to your mobile phone, that you can kill off at the end of your campaign. You'll pay for each call that's diverted to you but they're not very expensive and you probably won't get many calls. It's good to offer people an easy way to get in touch with you. Most 1300 number companies also offer message services, so a real person can answer on your behalf then text you the message.

Nice-to-haves:

- A website – if you can get a domain with your name, that's perfect: www.yourname.com.au – then you'll also be able to create emails at that same address, which looks très professional. You can keep the site and use it for something else later if you don't get in. If you are elected, you can maintain it as

"Thank goodness you're here!"

your professional page for the role you've been elected to do. It's handy to own a domain that has your name on it.

- Business cards that you can leave with people – or make yourself a combo card/flyer/postcard.

- A graphic designer to create and set up your brand (even if you then look after it yourself), so everything you make uses the same fonts and colours.

- Social media designs: different platforms ask for images in different sizes and formats, so you might need to make a square profile pic, a long narrow banner for a page, and images of a particular size to go on to your posts. You'll save a lot of time if you set up templates you can re-use.

Headshots and other photos

Good photos are essential. Whether you take them yourself or pay someone to do them, make sure they're good ones. I talk about finding a professional photographer later in this section.

Get a variety of photos taken in different outfits and settings. Flattering, up-to-date photos will be useful during your campaign and afterwards. You might find it handy to have photos of you drinking coffee, walking your dog or training your stunt cow (photos with animals are winners), reading a report, catching the bus, talking to someone, pointing at a boat … whatever shows the kinds of things that are important to you. Then you can bang these onto brochures or your website at short notice.

Your campaign photos should make you look like you usually do, only slightly better. Basically, you want people to think, 'Oh, they look nice,' and 'They look like they could do the job of <whatever you're trying to get elected to do>'.

Tip: Dress for your photos the way you would for a job interview since that's effectively what an election campaign is.

Whether you do or don't look the same as most of the other candidates who are likely to stand for your particular election, find your own version of the 'uniform' for the job you're applying for, and wear that in your photos. See Chapter 1: Your appearance and Chapter 4: What to wear for more on this.

➡ What's a headshot?

A headshot needs to show your head and top part of your shoulders – up close, not from a distance.

To find examples of poses, hairstyles, outfits and make-up that look good in photos, search online for headshots of actors and authors. There are also innumerable articles and videos on the internet about what to wear and how to pose. In general, the advice seems to be: wear simple necklines, avoid distracting spangly accessories and overly patterned or glitzy fabrics. And, if you're a make-up wearer, wear a little more make-up than usual, focusing attention on your eyes or mouth. If you have a high forehead or are bald, you might like to use some translucent powder to take off any shine.

You can take your own photos. Most smartphones take high resolution images. Again, search the internet for tips. It'll require some patience and ingenuity, but you can do a lot with a white bedsheet as a backdrop, some household lamps and white paper as reflectors. Most smartphones can take photos using a timer, so you can do it without help, if necessary.

I've tried all the various options: taking my own photos, getting help from a friend, and hiring a professional photographer. I've had mixed results from all of these. However, I think it's most time-effective to find a photographer who takes the kinds of photos I like, and who I feel comfortable with. They smarten up the pix, remove background distractions and then provide them in a form that's useful to my graphic designer.

Many photographers can show up anywhere with all their gear, including backdrops and lights, take shots inside and outside, let you change outfits as many times as you like

"Thank goodness you're here!"

in the time available, then send you an agreed number of touched-up photos afterwards.

Get inside shots done against a plain white background. That'll make it easier for someone (maybe you) to digitally remove the background so your photo can be overlain on different images. Many photographers will do this in Photoshop for you as part of the deal and send you an image with a transparent background.

Some people book a hair and/or beauty appointment before their shoot, if they're not confident to do it themselves. Some photographers can arrange a stylist as part of the shoot. See the Grooming and make-up section in this chapter for more ideas about this.

You want your headshot to look like you. As you look now.

→ Finding a good photographer

How do you find a good photographer? Ask for recommendations. This is a good opportunity to tell people that you're planning to stand for election. I'd advise you to tell everyone you talk to about your campaign, even if the thought makes you squirm.

Of course, well-meaning friends will recommend the person who photographed their Collie dog or their sister's cookbook, so you'll need to winnow those suggestions and try to find photographers who take great headshots. Of people.

If you can't get a recommendation, search the internet for photographers in your area who take corporate photos and look at their portfolios. Do you like their photos? If so, get in touch and ask for a quote.

Tip: You might find that it's cheaper to get your photos done at the same time as someone else, so if friends or family members also need headshots, you could include them in the booking. That could also make it feel slightly more fun, or less stressful.

Ways to use your photos

You'll want to be ready to quickly email off a photo any time you're asked for one. It's amazing how many times people want photos – if you'll be speaking at an event or talking to someone on the radio, event organisers will often ask for a high-resolution, decent photo of you. If you have a website, put high resolution photographs on it for the media to download, too.

You might like to make an email footer for your campaign emails that contains your headshot, or include a photo in your e-newsletter template.

Engaging a graphic designer or going it alone

When I say 'designer' I mean graphic designer. These are the people who make the things that represent you when you're not there. Designers often do branding work for people and companies, so finding someone who knows a lot about printing means they can save you a stack of time and money.

I estimate that you'll need to pay about A$1,500 to a designer to set you up for your campaign. This will get you some really solid basics that can be easily repurposed, be easily re-used or repurposed. When you're clear about potential voters you want to talk to and how you want to reach them, a designer can help you make a list of things to create (e.g. hard-copy postcards, billboards, signage for your vehicle, yard signs, a template for your e-newsletter and email signature, and templates for online events and social media posts). Then they can give you quotes and lead times to allow to make all those things.

You want to look successful from the start. Think about other people or businesses that you perceive as successful. I bet those businesses have nice signage outside their premises, their offices are colour coordinated and neat, their vehicles are sign-written (with no spelling mistakes and everything is clear to read), their websites look modern and, again, don't have any spelling mistakes or bloopers. I bet they usually dress well and keep their make-up and jewellery tasteful.

"Thank goodness you're here!"

This is all design and branding. They are doing all these things deliberately.

You can only be in one place at a time. Good branding lets you extend your presence and your message to a lot of other places. Design gets you and your vibe into the hands and minds and hearts of a huge number of people. When they see it repeatedly, they start to recognise and remember you. That's its purpose.

At some point your graphic designer will need all your contact details to put on to the things they're designing for you – business cards, flyers (if you want them) etc. Decide whether you'll be setting up a website or social media accounts, so you can include all those details on whatever you print. I'll talk some more about social media and websites in the following section.

If you're not sure about everything in your campaign, that's OK. I approached mine in an iterative way – getting ideas as I went along, then checking whether they fitted my main message, audience and budget.

When it comes to graphic design and printing, you can always get small digital print runs of things and you can shred paper and get it reprinted. Anything digital can be changed.

➡ Finding a good graphic designer

Choose a graphic designer by asking people you know. It'll be tempting to look for a student or someone's kid who's 'good with computers'. However, in my experience watching people go down this route, you'll end up with half a job done.

If you can't get a referral, find the peak body for graphic designers – in Australia this is the Australian Graphic Design Association (AGDA – www.agda.com.au) – and look for their member listings. Check out each designer's webpage and narrow it down to three choices. Phone or email each one. If you can't get hold of them easily, or they don't get back to you in a reasonable time, they might not be the best person for you. Many designers work alone or in small studios, so give them a few days to get back to you.

Find a graphic designer who does the kind of work you want – if you get someone who's managed corporate branding or election campaigns, they'll have the skills you need. Usually someone with a few years of experience will do a good, fast job for you.

Many graphic designers are good at specific things, so they might be terrific at designing wine labels or creating hand drawn lettering but take a long time to create what you need for your campaign.

If you know you'll be getting a lot of printing done, with signs and flyers etc, many printers have in-house graphic designers. This can be very cost-effective. Ask to see examples of their work.

If you're running a statewide or national campaign, there are companies who'll provide you with everything you need to promote yourself.

Going it alone?

The advantage of doing your own design is that it puts you in control.

If you have the skills and can do it well, you can make the things you imagine. But it's hard to know when to stop, and you can waste huge amounts of time fiddling around fixing your kerning. Or googling kerning.

I'd advise you not to do your own design unless you're a really good graphic designer. And even then, you really should be campaigning and meeting people. Spending time on your computer might be a form of advanced avoidance.

"Thank goodness you're here!"

That said, as I write this, there are platforms like Canva that allow you to set up your own branding and crank out designs for pretty much anything like business cards, flyers, banners for webpages, social media image templates ... Some graphic designers will set this up for you so you have your colours and fonts etc to re-use and keep your branding looking tight.

If you do your own design, resist the urge to keep experimenting and changing your templates every time you make anything – pick a look, a colour scheme, a set of fonts and use this throughout your whole campaign. You might get bored with it, but consistency is what'll help people to remember you.

Social media

Social media is extremely time-consuming. It can make you feel like you're being really productive, but there's no substitute, especially early in your campaign, for talking to human beings and listening to them to work out the kinds of things they're interested in.

Before you go nuts tweetling, face-chatting and book-tokking, remind yourself who you're aiming to talk to. What do they read? Do they use social media a bit or at all? Maybe you do have a pool of potential voters on a particular platform, but very few contacts with them.

Make your decisions about social media according to where your voters are.

Also consider using social media platforms where you already have a good network and where you're comfortable writing and sharing posts.

You can use software that allows you to write and schedule your social media posts on various platforms. This often allows you to make different versions of posts for different social media sites and to write things in a bunch and publish them regularly, so you seem highly organised.

I kept a list of all my potential blog and social media ideas and wrote and scheduled some of them to go with particular phases of my campaign. Posts were categorised so I could post regularly in a variety of ways. Each week I posted something about my council or my city, positive ideas from other cities that might work in my town, photos from my walks around the place, and an invitation to come to an event and chat to me.

Blog posts in particular take a long time to write. Even a short one can take hours. It's like writing an article or short story. That's why I caution people about thinking social media is easy. If you don't find writing easy, and you're not clear about what every single post is intended to do, you can waste a lot of time.

I wrote longer thought-pieces on my website's blog page. Then I linked to these in social media posts. I did this so I wouldn't lose my content if my social media accounts were closed for any reason, and I could also monitor how many people were reading the posts, visiting my site etc. I set up a pop-up on my site encouraging visitors to sign up to my mailing list.

It's OK to play the social media thing by ear in the first part of your campaign. If it's not working for you, either use it a lot less, schedule your posts so they're regular but further apart, or dump it entirely.

Working out a method of collecting contact information

As I flagged earlier, it's important to build your contact list throughout your campaign.

In the first instance, I think it's useful to export all your personal contacts from your phone or your email contact database into a spreadsheet and sort people into categories. As you go along in your campaign you might want to make a note each time you meet them and anything memorable you discuss, ie make a note each time you meet people, about anything memorable you discuss. Try to contact everyone several times during your campaign, several times during your campaign, rather than just seeing a lot of the people you like.

"Thank goodness you're here!"

see a handy template

Setting this spreadsheet up may be a good task to get a volunteer to help with. If you can afford to hire a temp or virtual assistant, they can probably put all this information together neatly in a single spreadsheet for you in no time flat.

Highlight any missing contact details – for example, if you later decide that you'll send everyone something in the post, then you'll need everyone's postal address. Easier to start collecting that info now than doing it at the last minute, right?

During your campaign, you'll want to build on your initial list. Invite people to be one of your contacts and treat them as part of your 'inner circle' group. Make it clear that your contacts will get exclusive information and invitations during your campaign. Let them know that they're special and valued.

Here are some ideas for capturing the contact details of people you meet.

You could ask for their business card, or hand people a notebook or sign-up sheet to write their details in. However, it's often hard to read people's writing, they might not give you the info you need, and it means transcribing it later.

You can type people's details into your phone or email contact list. However, it'll be hard to collect them all together later unless you tag or group them in some way.

I found it useful to get people to sign up to my e-newsletter, and I used my e-newsletter application as a kind of contacts database, as well as my Excel spreadsheet, as it collected people's email addresses.

To make it easier for people to sign up, most e-newsletter applications now let you set up a kind of app that you open on your smart phone or tablet device and it pops up a sign-up page for your e-newsletter.

Alternatively, you can open your website on your phone and ask them to type their details in the sign-up form there. Depending on how you've set that up, it'll send them an automated confirmation email so they can give you permission to contact them.

Add sign-up buttons to your social media accounts. Invite people to join up and receive your e-newsletter.

People running large campaigns sometimes use customer relationship management (CRM) software, but I think the cost and the learning curve would far outweigh any benefits for a smaller campaign.

Keeping in touch via e-newsletters

An e-newsletter is a fancy name for a group email. You can use e-newsletters to send people information they might not know, ask them for advice and invite them to events.

One way to send e-newsletters is by creating a group using your normal email software (make sure you put all the names into the BCC – blind carbon copy – field so no-one can see anyone else's name or email address).

However, I think it's easier to use an e-newsletter marketing site, import your list of contacts there (from your spreadsheet), and use their great-looking templates to easily create more 'newslettery-looking' e-newsletters.

You might live in a part of the world where emails sent to mailing list need to contain a clear method that allows them to unsubscribe – this is usually a link at the bottom of the email. E-newsletter sites include these features automatically.

The other advantage of using e-newsletter sites is that you can see how many people open your messages and whether they click on links, so you can decide whether to keep making the effort or not.

If you're writing e-newsletters as part of your communication plan, schedule them, work out which messages you need to include at different phases of your

"Thank goodness you're here!"

campaign, and always invite people to click Reply to talk to you directly. Your plan and list of topic ideas will make it so much easier to know what to write about – you can re-use ideas and photos from your e-newsletter in your social media posts and vice versa.

It can take several hours to half a day to write a good e-newsletter, so make them as effective as possible by making them personal and chatty, and telling the person who'll be reading it why it's important to get you elected and how they can do small things to help you. For example, you might include a poll or an invitation to contact you and tell you what they think about particular issues, or invite them to forward your email to friends and family.

Add a line at the bottom of your e-newsletter encouraging anyone who receives a copy forwarded from a friend to sign up themselves (and that way you'll have them on your contact list so you can reach them directly).

➜ Why bother with e-newsletters?

I think e-newsletters are great for situations when:

- your potential recipients are likely to vote for you and they read their emails and you can get their email addresses and permission to email them

- these people would otherwise be hard to reach because they're not keen on social media and they're not going to hear from you in other ways

- you think recipients might forward your messages to their friends and family

- you want to offer special events or meet-ups that are exclusive to these 'inner circle' people

- you want to talk to people in a personal way that's different to the way you'd write to the general public.

Flyers or brochures

The traditional election flyer is one that people put straight into the recycling bin, unless it's really terrible, in which case they guffaw over it with members of their household, mock it online and then throw it into the recycling bin.

Some people like the idea of letterboxing and distributing flyers because it's something they can achieve – they can fill weeks writing a flyer, then get boxes of flyers delivered and gee up their friends and family to trudge around town on their evenings and weekends putting them into letterboxes. You might even get to print out maps to guide their efforts.

If you're doing a big budget campaign, you can organise for your flyers to be delivered by your mail carrier or printing company to the suburbs you nominate.

I get it. It's very tangible and satisfying to produce bits of paper telling people to vote for you. It feels like you're doing what you're 'supposed' to do to get elected. However, unless your unsolicited flyer is outstanding, innovative and incredibly compelling (look, honestly, most aren't) most people will treat it like junk mail.

What makes a terrible flyer terrible? Two things: bad design and total self-absorption.

Badly designed terrible flyers look like they were made using Microsoft Word clip art. They often have writing covering every spare centimetre, usually in an old-fashioned font like Times New Roman, and lots of shouty demands for you to VOTE 1 FOR THIS PERSON. The colours can be hard to look at or read. The photos look blurry and dodgy. They could be selling carpet cleaning services or pizza. It's hard to tell. Keep your design plain and simple, with lots of white space.

The self-absorption issue is a tricky one. How do you tell people about yourself without talking too much about yourself? I talk about how to do this in the next section. For now, take my word for it that potential readers don't want to read about your 42 qualifications starting with the botany award you got in Grade 4.

"Thank goodness you're here!"

61

OK, you're determined to make a flyer – let's make it the best it can be

Punching out a million terrible, generic, Me Me Me-style flyers to bang into strangers' letterboxes isn't a good strategy. Does this mean you shouldn't make any kind of flyer? Nope. They can be useful if they have a clear purpose and they talk to the right people in a way that feels personal and relevant.

Focus on the reader, not on yourself.

Focus your flyers or brochures or postcards on the prospective voter who'll be reading them. Talk about things they care about. Tune in to their hopes, aspirations or frustrations. Sound like someone who values them and their opinions.

I talked about this in Chapter 3: Your people and Chapter 4: Getting your stuff together.

You might be thinking, 'But when do I tell them about myself? I need to persuade them to vote for me!'

I've got two things to say about this. First, it's more effective to show rather than tell. Second, as everyone's grandma will tell you, if you want to be interesting, then be interested.

How do you show people what's important to you, and what kind of person you are, without telling them directly?

1. Talk to one person – the person reading your words will feel more connected to you if you write as though you're talking just to them, rather than to a whole group. That's how I've written this book. I've written it for you.

2. Show what you want, not what you don't want – paint a picture (in words, images or actual paintings, if you like) of the sort of community, workplace or world you'd like to live in. Talk about the opportunities and possibilities you see for your group, school or town. Focus on what's positive and possible, rather than stimulating fear or disgust.

"Thank goodness you're here!"

3. Ask questions about a topic that's close to their hearts (and yours too, by association).

4. Offer to help people get their problems solved with the organisation you're trying to get elected to. Even though you're not in the 'job' yet, act like you are. You can still take people's issues to an organisation even if you're not an elected representative.

5. Give examples of how the thing you're proposing works in other places (so long as your potential voters don't dislike those places).

All of these things show people what you value and what kind of person you are.

Ask questions. Ask if what you propose sounds good to the reader. Ask if you've missed something. Invite them into a conversation with you. Even if they don't respond, they'll feel good that you asked. Asking makes you seem open, approachable and interested.

Let's talk about how an effective flyer can make a reader know, feel or do things (or all three).

Know: talk about things that will appeal to a potential voter.

Think about your whole campaign and decide where a flyer or series of flyers might fit into the different phases. What do you want people to know about?

When I get a flyer I think 'What is this about?', then 'Who is this from?'

Make sure your flyer answers both those questions quickly.

Aim your flyer squarely at the person reading it, so it's all about them, not all about you. Pick a topic that'll interest them. Make this the main subject of the flyer. Include your details but make them of secondary importance. Someone should see the subject they care about, then see your name, photo and contact details.

You want someone to read your flyer and see your name and think, for example, 'Ah, this is an invitation to hear about saving endangered ducks in my neighbourhood! Who sent it? Oh, right, it's from Josephina Bloggs. They must care about ducks as much as I do. And look, they're standing for the Duck Appreciation Committee election in June.'

You showed them what you cared about, you didn't tell them.

Other examples of showing rather than telling:

Invite the reader to a community tree-planting event and give them a little story or some facts about the success of past planting events. They'll assume you're an active community member who loves nature. Ask their opinion on dangerous conditions in their industry and include your thoughts on what you'd like to see happening. You'll sound like an informed and determined person who intends to make a difference. List all the great things students at your school can do, thanks to previous student representatives. This makes you seem motivated and like someone who promotes the achievements of others.

Use a flyer to let people know what you care about, by focusing on what they care about.

Feel: make me say Aww, Hahahaha or Hmmm.

Make your flyer lovely, funny, arresting or thought-provoking. Think about what might make someone keep it or stick it on their fridge or pass it along to a friend. If you stimulate their feelings and make something keep-able, it's more likely that they'll remember you at voting time.

What makes marketing material keep-able? Hint: it usually doesn't have an enormous picture of someone's smiling mug and 'Vote 1' on the front.

Work out what might promote one of the messages behind your election campaign. Consider using beautiful or striking artwork, pictures of animals or local scenes, or inspiring or even amusing quotes. Do what's appropriate for you and your potential voters. If your platform is about toxic waste dumps, then cute kitten pix or hilarious quotes might send the wrong message.

Note: if you're going to write quotes, write something people have never read before, don't pull something from a book of inspirational (yawn) quotes. Write something you've thought of or quote a phrase from your favourite book (make sure you attribute it). Do I need to say that the quote should reflect something about your campaign or your values? Write quotes and text using the font you use for all your campaign materials. Put your contact details on the back or somewhere discreet, like in a margin.

I made postcards with humorous, catchy writing on the front to remind readers about the power they had as voters. They would assume this was also my perspective. I included some information on the back about myself; however, this was still aimed at the reader. I hoped these cards would be amusing and attractive enough for people to keep them and put on their fridge or by their desk, rather than dropping into the compost bin. I hoped they'd think of me each time they saw the postcard, and that they'd recognise my branding if they came across any of my other campaign material.

Do: encourage your potential voter to take some kind of action.

Think about things you can invite potential voters to do.

Use your flyer to invite people to come to an exciting event, sign up to your mailing list so they can hear about other interesting events, buy an attractive campaign t-shirt or cat collar, tell you their opinion on something that affects them, follow your socials so they can interact with other like-minded people, go to your website to learn more about a topic they care about ...

Help people to feel more connected and purposeful by suggesting things for them to do.

Anyone reading your action-focused flyer will associate your name and your go-getter-ishness with the hot topic you're talking about.

The ultimate aim of inviting people to Do all this Doing is to collect their contact details. Most online events and websites can be set up to invite people to add their contact details and give you permission to contact them. You're not being creepy – you want to invite them to future events, keep them up to date with the subject they care

"Thank goodness you're here!"

about and, most importantly, ask for their vote when the time comes. You're great, so they'll likely want to vote for you, but they might forget, so reminding them is in everyone's interest.

Harness the power of trust. Set up a personal distribution network.

Think about who's going to deliver or distribute your campaign materials. Yes, you could get a marketing company to distribute them to recycling bins across your region.

Wait. That sounded negative. What I mean is, they'll go into hundreds of mailboxes of people who don't know or care about you and THEY'LL bung 'em into the bin.

Think about getting your beautiful, memorable flyers into the right hands. Who is likely to read your flyers? Someone whose delightful, trustworthy friend or family member gives them one, along with a little story about why it's important.

Invite your supporters to be your distribution network. Tell them what a huge difference they can make with a small effort.

If you read Chapter 3: Your people you'll know who your prospective voters are, you'll know who's in your close network of contacts and you'll know that I advocate talking to people in personal ways.

Recommendations from friends and families carry far more weight than impersonal mass-produced marketing. Even people who don't care about politics are more likely to tune in and maybe even vote after a personal recommendation.

What could be more personal than your Aunty Shirley or your favourite wholefoods store owner giving you a flyer, telling a story and even asking for your vote, saying: 'This person wants to reduce rents for local businesses in this area. I'd love it if you'd consider supporting them. The election is next month.'

How many people do you need to reach? How many of your friends and family might be willing to hand out your campaign materials?

How many flyers would they need to hand out for you? Do the maths. I told supporters that if they gave out 10 of my postcards to 10 friends, and asked for their votes, they could get me elected.

That seemed doable.

Make it a small ask and a small task for someone to hand out your flyers. Plan to give willing supporters small packs of your flyers and tell them the story you want them to repeat. Thank them. Keep in touch with them. Ask if they'd like some more and keep on giving them suggestions about people they might give them to.

Make sure all of your supporters are on your list of very special people to contact just before voting time. Thank them again. Ask them if they'd reach out to all their networks, including people they might have given your flyers to, to ask them to vote.

Don't forget that you need to be giving flyers out at every chance you get as well.

I talk more about giving out flyers in the Chapter 5: Campaigning nitty gritty – and other, better ways to get your campaign information into the world.

Keep track of how many flyers are going out – this is a good way of gauging your potential reach and the progress of your campaign.

Signs and posters

Signs and posters can be expensive and time-consuming to plan, have printed, find sites for, put up, maintain and take down to store or dispose of. They end up being fairly generic and highly ignorable because it's hard to make them personal.

Gee, I sound pretty negative about signs and posters, don't I? I've helped with a lot of campaigns and seen how much time they can chew up. If they're part of your campaign because you believe they'll encourage your voters to vote for you, and you have the budget and time for them, then great.

"Thank goodness you're here!"

If your campaign plan is built around getting the votes you need by spending your time talking to people in personal ways, then forget about signs. Bear in mind that you still might feel panicky and have misgivings when other people start putting up signs. But feel the panicky misgivings and rest assured that you're doing what you think will work for you.

Signs

Signs include yard signs, billboards, ads on taxis or buses. You can also advertise by putting signs on trailers, sandwich boards, poles or even rubbish bins, or by sign-writing vehicles.

Check the rules about signs for your election campaign. Some have strict rules about the types, sizes and numbers of signs you can have, dates they can be displayed and places they can be displayed. Some elections limit the amount of money you're allowed to spend on various kinds of election materials. Rules might also stipulate what information you need to put on signs, for example, the name and address of the person authorising them.

If you're standing for a major state or federal election, or for a political party, signs serve a few purposes. They help the party to advertise their brand and they identify you as being part of that brand, which might guide party-faithful types to vote for you. Most major parties have someone to coordinate the printing of the signage. You won't get a lot of say about what goes onto the signs. Even if you're standing as part of a political party, there's a high chance you'll still be responsible for getting volunteers to put the signs up and take them down. Or doing it yourself with your Uncle Sami.

These are the major steps involved in yard-sign-wrangling:

- Once you know the size and number of signs you're allowed, get quotes from printers who do this kind of work.

    o How much lead time will they need from the time you give them the artwork, to when the signs will be ready for collection?

- What format will they need for the artwork (pictures and words for the sign)?

- Where will the printed signs be ready for collection?

- How will they be packaged? You'll need to plan for a suitable vehicle to pick them up if they're bundled into a great big pile.

- Find fences, walls or yards where you want to put up your signs and get permission from the owners. This is time-consuming! You need to keep these people on side before, during and after your campaign. If your sign blows down or is damaged, you want them to let you know. Don't bother putting up signs in cul-de-sacs or not-very-visible places, it's a waste of time, money and effort.

- Once you know how many signs you have locations for, book in the printing with the printer ahead of time. Every other candidate will be trying to have signs printed at the same time as you.

- Schedule time into a calendar for you or a trusted volunteer to coordinate the collection/storage/erection of the signs. They'll need to look at each site to plan and buy or assemble materials to fix them in place in different situations – think wooden or metal stakes, drills with spare batteries, screws, wire, cable ties, hammers and a contact sheet to leave with property owners so they can get in touch about sign-related issues.

- Schedule time post-election for signs to be taken down, transported and stored or disposed of. Again, check any rules that apply to your election. You might be fined for leaving your signs up too long.

- Design your signs so they can be easily read and understood from a distance.

- Get someone picky to double-check the designs in case you spelled VOTE or your name incorrectly, and all required information is on there.

- Send the designs to the printer and confirm that they received them.

- Approve any proofs the printers send you – get them double-checked again by someone who's not you.

"Thank goodness you're here!"

69

Posters

Posters are a similar deal to signs. They can be easier to wrangle than yard signs (and wrangling the owners of yards where you'd like to put up signs) and help you to reach specific groups of people at places they go to. You can do small print runs to create a range of different posters for different audiences.

But the thing with posters is: you need somewhere to put them.

Dedicate some time to working out where you're allowed to put them, what size they need to be, and design them so they are eye-catching and memorable to a passer-by who probably isn't a passionate reader of political posters.

Depending on where you live, you might not be able to stick up posters wherever you like. Your election might have rules that consider posters to be the same as other kinds of signs, restricting the size and number of them.

You need to have people to put your posters up, replace them if they're damaged and take them down at the end of your campaign.

See the steps in the previous section about how to get signs out into the world. This is much the same for posters. You'll need to create the artwork, get them printed, transport and store them, have the materials and a plan for putting them up, get approval (in some cases) to put them up and arrange for them to be replaced if they're damaged (or stolen, if they're AMAZING and steal-worthy).

I did make posters, but I gave them to people to have at home or wherever they wanted, not for them to be put up in public. That was a weird but surprisingly personal and effective strategy. I talk about my poster a little more in Chapter 7: Anatomy of my campaign.

Websites

Depending on the size of your election, a website is an excellent way people can find you and check you out. You might choose to set up a social media page and use that instead of creating your own website; however, for any kind of election a website can look professional.

Your website can be as simple as just one page with a photo and some text and contact details – basically it's like an online flyer.

Anything that involves technology will take longer than you ever imagined and will result in frustration. Do you have a family member or close friend who would be able to help you set up a site and emails? I'd usually caution against this, but it can be tricky to find reliable professionals to do it for you. If you can't get a recommendation, you might be better off with a skilled friend. Learning to do this yourself isn't hard but it's time-consuming and you might prefer to just get on with your job of campaigning.

Some designers can create a mock-up of a website (a picture of what it looks like) and some can create the site for you, or they know someone who can. Expect to pay many hundreds of dollars to set up a basic site and several hundred dollars a year to have it hosted.

Make sure that anyone who makes you a website gives you all the information you need to look after it yourself. You need registration information and logins. Keep them somewhere safe. When this is all over, you'll need to take everything down again.

Also bear in mind the electoral rules about what needs to be written on all your advertising in certain periods of the campaign. You might need to add a sentence to the bottom of your website, for example, saying who authorised the site. You need to know how to do this, or who can do this for you when you need it.

➡ **What should you have on your website?**

Simple is often best. Think about why someone might come to your site – what do they want to know?

They'll be visiting because they've either heard about you and want to check you out, or they want to get in touch with you.

Have a terrific photo on your site. If you'll need them to recognise your face as well as your name when they vote, use the same photos you'll include with your candidate statement.

"Thank goodness you're here!"

71

Include your name prominently, possibly written the same way it'll appear on the voting form. Try to form the strongest possible association between you and the information they'll see when they vote.

Then think about other things your site can do:

- Tell visitors about your campaign.

- Invite readers to get in touch or come to events so they can get to know you in person and share their thoughts with you.

- Ask people to sign up to your e-newsletter or contacts database, so they'll get special invitations and information.

- Give media representatives information about you – make a special part of your site aimed at them. Write a summary bio you'd be happy to see reproduced in the paper or used to introduce you on a radio program and provide them with downloadable, high quality photos. This will save them and you the effort of requesting/ sending info and photos.

- Set up your site so it automatically displays your social media posts or lists your latest blog posts.

- Display invitations to events with links to RSVP or get more info.

Writing a winning candidate statement

Not every type of election campaign requires you to write a formal statement, but lots do. Some also require a headshot photo to accompany the statement, which is why I've banged on about the importance of getting a good photo and using it throughout your campaign.

It might be the case that the only thing a prospective voter ever sees or knows about you is contained in your candidate statement.

Therefore, this is your big chance to get as many extra votes as you can from people who've otherwise never heard of you.

My suggestions for writing a great statement are:

- Check the rules, so you know how many words or characters you're allowed to write, and when it has to be submitted.

- Look at statements from previous elections, if you can find them (I found these for local Tasmanian council elections on the Tasmanian Electoral Commission website).

  - Work out which candidates you'd have voted for and which ones make you say 'Nope' – think about why this is. Do they have weird or out-of-date photos? Are they talking about themselves too much in their statement? Really focus on the things that put you off and make sure you don't do those things.

- If you can leave line breaks between your paragraphs, do that, so what you write is clear and easy to read.

- Focus on the reader and what they'll get by voting for you, rather than focusing on yourself and how ace you are.

- Focus on positive things and what's possible for you to accomplish in the elected role, without being too aspirational and pie-in-the-sky.

- Use short sentences without too many long words.

- Try to sound like a warm, relatable human being and don't be afraid of using some gentle humour.

- Don't forget to ask for people's vote. Be explicit. 'I'd love your number 1 vote.'

For ideas on writing in a human voice, see my tips in Chapter 4: Getting your stuff together.

Write several versions if you like, making sure the word count is perfect for each one. This way, if everything falls apart before the deadline for putting in your statement, or if your website needs

"Thank goodness you're here!"

something or the media needs some words, you've got a range to choose from.

Tick it off your list.

(Yes, you might revisit it later but it's fine for now.)

See Chapter 7: Anatomy of my campaign for the bio and photo I ended up using. I'd probably write it differently today, but it fitted my campaign at the time.

➡ Writing about yourself is uncomfortable

It always is. It might take you a few go-rounds to nail it. You might never completely love what you've written. Look at it this way: your statement isn't actually for you anyway – it's for a stranger to read it and think, 'They sound nice/smart/ credible' and 'I can imagine them doing this role.'

One way to do it is by weaving in your credentials while focusing on likely voters and things they care about.

Say you can see easy ways to immediately improve local water quality because you've worked as a hydrologist for 15 years. Tell readers that you want to see more kids riding bikes to school because you're a primary school teacher who sees the environmental and health benefits. Describe how increasing wages and conditions in your industry will positively affect your colleagues and the community. Mention that your interest in botany started way back in your wonderful Girl Guide group, and how this led to a recent discovery of rare species in a local park.

Writing about yourself is uncomfortable. There's no getting around it. If you're really stuck, get someone else to write your candidate statement for you and then edit what they write.

"Thank goodness you're here!"

A word about podcasts

If you dislike writing and love chatting, you might be tempted to start a podcast. They can seem deceptively easy if you listen to really slick ones.

What you might not realise is that professional podcasters have a team of people helping to plan, write, direct and then edit every episode. Even non-professional podcasters spend many hours on every episode. They often, but not always, buy good microphones and use special software for editing and publishing. Adding show notes and links, which is valuable to people who find your podcast and who might want the information without listening, is even more time-consuming. Poor sound quality, background noise or an unfocused approach will quickly put people off listening.

You also have to find a way to promote your podcast to get people to listen to it. How much lead time do you have before your election?

I'm not saying don't do a podcast, I'm suggesting that you weigh up the benefits against the time, money and effort you'll be expending.

A much better bet would be to get yourself invited onto someone else's podcast. Make sure you choose one that your target voters listen to, and allow for the fact that the podcaster might record their episodes months in advance.

Don't forget about radio. Radio is a powerful, immediate way to reach people. Sure, you won't get all the time in the world to talk the way you would on a podcast, but if you know your potential voters listen to particular stations, it's a great, low-cost way to reach them.

I talk more about this in Chapter 5: Getting traditional media.

"Thank goodness you're here!"

What to wear

Think about your appearance as part of your brand. Does the way you dress reassure people that you could do the job you're trying to get elected to do? (I talked about this in Chapter 1: Your appearance.)

While your character is the most important part of you, most people will initially only have your appearance to go by when they're working out what they think about you.

Can you give them a way to remember you? For example, if you have branding colours for your campaign, you might repeat these colours in most of your outfits, for example with a scarf or tie or piece of clothing.

Try to always dress slightly better than you think you should, as you'll be meeting and talking to people everywhere you go.

Of course, you also need to live your life and walk your dog and feed your alpacas and drop off your Dad's old Australian Geographic magazines to the tip shop, so you're not going to dress in 'campaign clothes' all the time. But at least wear your newer King Gees to the tip shop, the ones that don't show your bum cleavage when you squat down. If you're doing your grocery shopping, wear nice jeans rather than daggy sweatpants. Dress a step or two better than you usually would.

To summarise this section: reduce the amount of effort it takes to look presentable by pre-planning sure-fire good outfits and having them handy. Assemble accessories and other campaign materials so you can grab them and go. Get good haircuts regularly and keep yourself clean and neat.

Assemble some sure-fire outfits

If you're not the kind of person who usually spends much time thinking about what you wear, you might find it stressful to have to dress at short notice to attend a campaigning event.

I've talked to a few people who are 'in the public eye' and asked for their suggestions on low-stress campaign dressing (I mean, no 'added' stress):

- 'Try on anything you think you'll wear for your campaign to make sure it fits and doesn't have any stains or loose threads. Fix that stuff ahead of time so you're not panicking at the last minute or showing up looking untidy.'

- 'You need to be comfortable, especially when it comes to your feet. Get comfortable shoes.'

- 'If you have to go to events that could be outside, make sure you've got appropriate shoes to change into. There's nothing worse than watching someone teetering and tottering through dirt wearing office shoes.'

- 'Take the time to assemble a couple of great outfits. Take a photo of them, so you can get dressed quickly without standing in front of the wardrobe.'

- 'I've got one entire outfit hanging at home, with everything there: undies, shoes, tops, bottoms, jacket, scarf, jewellery, make-up, comb and hair product. I know I can just grab the whole lot and get changed somewhere.'

- 'I have one good blazer. I always have it with me. It's cream, so it looks smart and, even when I'm not very dressed up, makes me look the part.'

- 'Wear plain, neat clothes most of the time and keep brightly coloured earrings, necklace, a patterned scarf and lipstick handy, so you can throw them on and look more dressed up.'

- 'I like pink, so I made sure I was wearing at least one pink thing during my entire campaign. It became my brand. People knew I was the one in pink.'

- 'Keep your shoes in good shape. People notice shoes. They don't need to be fashionable – definitely go for comfort over style – but make sure they're not scuffed or worn.'

- 'Don't wear jangly or noisy things – the sounds can irritate people and really stuff up the sound quality if you're being interviewed.'

"Thank goodness you're here!"

Grooming and make-up

People look for clues about how much you keep up with the modern world based on subtle things like current (but not tragically current) eyebrow shapes, make-up and hairstyles. I'm not saying it's a reliable way to judge someone's skills, but if you haven't changed your hairstyle or what you wear for 10 or 15 years, some people might assume your ideas and information are equally dated.

I can't say this enough – you want people to really see you when they see your photo or talk to you, which means you want them to focus on your mouth and eyes when you talk. This is why I advise people to remove or minimise anything others might find distracting. That's my opinion – do what suits you and the kinds of people who'll vote for you.

An easy way to make your eyes a focus is to have bushy brows trimmed by a barber, or tweezed, threaded or waxed by a beautician. If you have light coloured lashes, consider tinting (dyeing) them. This will make your eyes look clear and open without mascara or eyeliner. It'll last for about six weeks. You can get kits to do it yourself or get a professional to do it, if you're scared of going blind from the chemicals, which is a reasonable fear.

If you are happy with your brows au naturel, then leave them. Maybe comb them neatly for photos and outings though, so your hairs aren't waving at people. If you have a beard, unless it's your key identifying feature, try not to let it seem more interesting than you are. Give it a comb or a trim. In terms of displaying body hair or body parts, ask yourself if you'd show them at a job interview. If not, maybe keep them to yourself during your campaign. It's up to you.

➡ **Non make-up make-up for people who want their skin to look a bit better**

Anyone can make their face and mouth look slightly smoother and more 'groomed' with tinted moisturiser and lip balm.

Quite a few brands now do unisex tinted moisturiser or something similar, sometimes called CC creams, to hide red patches or dark under-eye circles. You can make your own by mixing a few drops of foundation that matches your colouring into your sunscreen.

If you're getting photos done, ask the photographer if there's anything you can do beforehand to make your skin look smooth. They can often suggest a powder or tinted cream used by people who work in film or television. Whatever you use, blend it out into your hairline and around your eyes so it looks like your skin.

Many people in the public eye use a bronzer stick or a subtle blush on their face. You'll find lots of videos on the internet about using these to look healthy without looking made-up.

Jewellery and accessories

Accessories can be a terrific way to show your personality, even when you're dressing to show people that you understand and are prepared to do the job you're campaigning for.

Pick jewellery that makes you feel confident. Don't bother with anything you're not comfortable with. You'll seem less confident if you're constantly fiddling with what you're wearing.

Draw attention to your face by wearing things on your top half in colours that make your eyes look good or give you colour in your cheeks. Look for flattering colours in tops, jackets, scarves, earrings, crowns or feathered headdresses (if appropriate). Boldly-coloured clothing or accessories can make you memorable and allow you to be spotted from across a room.

→ Look like 'somebody'

If you want to walk into a room and look like 'somebody', dress as though you're already doing the role you're trying to be elected for, wearing something that fits the expected 'uniform' but with your own twist. If your prospective colleagues all wear suit jackets, you can look equally professional but steal the show with a tailored white, cream or brightly coloured blazer. Just one unexpectedly coloured or textured piece of your outfit – a tie, scarf, socks, amazing shoes – can set you apart.

The other thing that makes you look like somebody is to walk into a room and tell yourself as you walk in, 'I'm someone and I've ARRIVED'. Pause in the doorway and take your time to look around as though you're looking for someone, give a big smile to your imaginary friend (or a real one, if you see one) and walk across the room as though you have an entourage following you.

If you're thinking, 'That won't work for me because I'm not very tall,' think again. It's nothing to do with height. It's about acting as though you belong there. Taking time. Taking up room. Just pause then enter the room.

Become someone who gives fabulous introductions. It's a generous thing to do, it gives you a task when you're feeling all at sixes and sevens, and it makes you seem like a gracious host, even when it's not your event. People love being introduced in ways that make them feel wonderful. Learn from other people's introductions or google for articles to tell you how to be a brilliant introducer.

Learn to stop touching your face, hair, earrings, cuffs etc when you're in public. It looks twitchy and makes you seem insecure. If, like me, you tend to self-soothe by touching your face, redirect the impulse and gently cup one hand inside the other when you're around other people. This makes you look relaxed and attentive, while giving your hands something to do so they don't run riot.

Here's my big style (and life) tip: if you repeat something it'll look like you did it on purpose. Do it once and it seems like an accident.

The easiest way to create an 'outfit' is to repeat something. If you have a pink jacket, wear pink somewhere else in your outfit. Silver spectacle frames? Add a silver ring and/or chose a bag with silver fittings.

You don't need to match exactly. Got lime green in the pattern of your blouse? Add greenish earrings. Warm whisky tones in your tie? That'll look good with your warm brown pleather satchel and your natty mustard hatband.

For minimalists or people who just don't care about what they wear

You can be a minimalist and still make sure you'll be remembered on voting day.

Here's how to assemble some appropriate clothes and accessories, so you don't have to make decisions each time you get dressed.

1. Choose plain, good quality outfits and add patterned scarves or shirts to draw attention to your face.

   Patterns with more than one colour in them (rather than just shades of blue, for example) go with more things and are easier to accessorise. Pick a colour from the pattern and repeat it somewhere else and you've got yourself a nice-looking outfit.

2. Have a 'thing'. People will remember you more easily if they associate you with a particular 'thing' you always have with you, like a splendid sparkly walking aid, a dapper hat, accessories in your signature colour, interesting brooches or a recognisable hair colour or style. You've always got your hair with you.

   Choose a 'thing' you're happy for people to comment on. Starting conversations is hard, so it's nice to make it easier for everyone. I think it's charming to compliment someone on their 'thing' they've obviously spent some effort on, chosen to wear

"Thank goodness you're here!"

or brought with them. I rarely comment on someone's body or anything about their appearance they don't have any control over.

3. Use your hair as an accessory by wearing shoes, a bag and belt in a similar colour. If you cover your hair or head, match your accessories to your covering. If you're bald, repeat your skin colour in shoes, bag and/or belts. Repeating your hair colour a few times in your outfit is a low-effort way of immediately looking pulled-together.

4. Your hair style should frame your face and bring attention to your eyes and your mouth, so people listen to what you say. If you have really memorable hair, then make a feature of it. If you have natural hair, wear it proudly and make sure your overall appearance says 'I understand this job and can do it'. A good haircut or style sends the message that you're organised, you pay attention to details and you respect yourself.

I've heard curly-haired people say they believe they're taken less seriously in a corporate environment. Yes, you could straighten it or style it so it's less of a feature. Or you could decide to dress in a way that fits the role you're aspiring to, and leave your hair the way you like it. If the role you're aspiring to has always been done by someone who looks very different to you, perhaps you're the person to show that different kinds of people are just as credible.

People of all genders have hair issues. If you're losing your hair or it's sparse because of a medical condition or treatment, talk to a hairdresser and tell them how you want to be perceived for your election. Take their advice about a style that'll make you look confident and credible, up close and from a distance. They see a lot of heads in their business. A super-short cut will take everyone's attention off your wispy bits and create a focus on your eyes and face. Some people love using a well-made wig, which makes every day a great hair day.

Don't forget the power of wearing stylish hats or scarves. I know two politicians who are instantly recognisable across a crowded room because of their headwear – the style of hat they each choose has become their trademark. Their hats also stop their heads from getting sunburned when they're at outside events. They're practical and an effective 'thing'.

Keep packs of campaign materials handy to grab and go

Your campaign materials aren't something you wear, but you do need to make sure you have them with you at all times.

Keep some packs of campaign materials with your campaign jacket or outfit, along with a notepad and pen, so you grab those when you get dressed.

You should be giving them to everyone you talk to and asking for their vote. Stop squirming – if they're enjoying the conversation with you, they'll be interested to hear that you're planning to stand for election.

Useful skills to start developing

There are quite a few skills that'll make your life easier while you're campaigning and when you're elected. Doing courses or workshops is a terrific way to meet people and tell them about your election.

See if you can find a way to learn how to have difficult conversations or handle mediations or negotiations. Sometimes Adult Education classes list these among their offerings. Otherwise, trained counsellors can teach you. I was a Lifeline telephone counsellor for a time – theirs was the best training I've ever had in how to regulate my own emotions and stay present with someone having a very difficult time.

Learn how to use your mobile phone properly:

- Protect it with a strong password or PIN.
- Learn how to create contacts quickly and send someone your contact details (yep, most phones will send yours at the click of a button).
- Learn how to send and receive text messages.
- Learn how to block calls.
- Set up Do Not Disturb times when, you guessed it, you don't want to be disturbed. You can make exceptions for people you really want to be disturbed by.

"Thank goodness you're here!"

- Learn how to mute your phone quickly without looking at it.

- Set up emails on your phone (if you want to see what's coming in while you're away from your computer). I suggest that you change your phone's settings to remove the automatic 'sent from my iPhone' or similar message that appears by default on every email. Note: my editor thinks you could keep those words if you're an inaccurate typist or have big fingers, so recipients will cut you some slack with your typos.

- Learn how to take photos on your phone and post them to social media.

Keep your contacts list updated. I made one in Excel after dumping out all my contacts from my Contacts database and phone records. It's worthwhile working out how to create a single list of contacts that's shared between all your devices, if you haven't already done this.

Learn to set up rules in your email program – getting on top of emails is a huge part of what you'll be doing, as you need to get back to people quickly. Setting up rules to file important things about your campaign and divert unimportant things frees up a lot of thinking space.

Set up your online calendar so you can use it with your phone and all your other devices – you'll live and die by your calendar as events pile up. I put everything time-dependent in mine, including reminders to phone or email people. You need to be able to rely on your phone calendar while you're out and to put in appointments as soon as they come up.

Learn how to write better, especially for social media – social media writing gets straight to the point, which is good for any kind of writing. You can often find online courses.

Learn to touch type – this will make all your communications much easier, and the amount of reading and note-taking you'll do if you get in will be hugely improved. Think how imposing you'll seem, fixing someone with your intelligent gaze while continuing to take notes as they talk.

Work on your public speaking or meeting skills – you might be amazed to know that there are groups who meet to work on public speaking skills and on how to run meetings. Search on the web or ask around. If you can speak more comfortably, then you can concentrate on what you need to say when the time comes to say something that's important to you.

Learn about meeting procedures in general, and, more specifically, about the meeting procedures for the organisation you want to join. Most decision-makers spend a lot of time in meetings. You'll even be asked to chair some of them. The rules about meeting procedures can seem archaic and overly formal (and sometimes boorrriiinnngg), but they're important to ensure that what is actually a room full of strangers with extremely different opinions can each be heard and make decisions. You've got a huge advantage if you know what's going on from the start of a new role. You can participate instead of wondering what's happening, when you're allowed to speak and why that man who snaps his underpants elastic each time he speaks has been allowed to speak twice. If you can find a mentor or someone to attend some meetings with you during your campaign, you'll get an idea of how the meetings work, and how much you'll need to learn so you can get off to a confident start once you're elected.

If you're creative, think about learning how to do your own graphic design with an online course or by becoming familiar with using one of the excellent online tools that'll help you make beautiful images and documents. You could also pay someone to teach you some basic skills one-on-one. I went a bit overboard and signed up for a one-year graphic design course at TAFE, mostly as professional development to add these skills to my communications business, but also because I hoped to do my own design during my campaign.

"Thank goodness you're here!"

Chapter 5

Campaigning nitty gritty

"Thank goodness you're here!"

When you made your plan you'll have thought about the people who are likely to vote for you, worked out what you'd like to say to them and, most importantly, how you'll say it so they hear it. That'll stop you from getting distracted by all the *excellent* suggestions everyone will have about making viral TwitFace memes.

To launch or not to launch?

I reckon a launch is important, even if it's a tiny event for you and a few friends. It's an important milestone and it makes your campaign feel real.

Get someone else to organise your launch, if it really gives you the yips.

If you can get someone with a public profile to launch you, that's even better. Send out a press release to invite the media to come along. Don't be sad if they don't. You can always put up blog posts, social media posts or send out an e-newsletter telling people about the event.

Yes, I do understand that a launch might feel more uncomfortable than a birthday party. At least no-one will sing at your launch. Hopefully. Unless you've written a theme song. In which case, I hope there's singing.

Tell everyone and ask for their vote

Explicitly tell everyone you talk to that you're standing for election and explicitly ask them for their vote.

People are most likely to remember you if they meet you in the flesh. When you meet someone, make the most of it. Be nice. LISTEN TO THEM. Whenever you get the chance, give them one of your business cards or your engaging postcards or flyers (that I know you'll keep crease-free in a special hard folder in your bag at all times) and always always always ask for their vote.

"Thank goodness you're here!"

'It's been great talking to you. I'm standing at the next election for XX. This is my card. I'd really love your vote.'

You don't need to thrust pamphlets into the hands of passers-by as if you're promoting your Melbourne Comedy Festival show, just don't miss a single opportunity.

If they say they don't live here, or try to return it, say, 'Hang on to it – do you know someone who lives here that you'd be willing to give it to?'

If they're really enthusiastic and supportive, say, 'Do you know other people who might vote? Can I give you a few to pass along?' and give them a few of your flyers. Invite them to join your mailing list, or add them yourself on the spot.

If they won't stop talking and you need to get away, point out your email address and say, 'I'd love to hear more about <whatever you were talking about> but I need to leave now. Would you be willing to send me an email?'

Then you'll have a chance to ask them if you can add them to your list of contacts.

➡ **Learn how your voting system works so you can explain it to people**

People will ask. And they'll expect you to know since you're pretty much applying for a job and need to know how the application process works.

Tip: If this makes you freak out, get a smart, logical friend to learn about it and summarise it for you. It's important to know how votes are counted. Consider writing a little explainer you can hand to people to explain how their vote will make a difference.

Keep building up your list of contacts

See Chapter 4: Working out a method of collecting contact information for suggestions on how to keep building up your list of contacts.

You want to keep adding names of people you can contact personally throughout your campaign. It's a good indicator of how many people you've successfully reached. Of course you'll reach lots of people, but it's powerful to look at your contact list and know who you're talking to, and that you can reach their friends and family through them.

Other campaigning methods are a lot like shouting into a tunnel – you have no idea who's listening or if they've heard you.

Plan how you'll ask your contacts to contact their contacts

The last phase of my campaign was devoted to asking everyone on my contact list if they'd contact a few people to ask their friends and family to vote for me. And to ask them to ask their friends and family. It relied on trust and recommendations.

I strongly recommend you consider doing this too. I'm not talking about the kinds of call centre setups that are used for large campaigns. I'm talking low-tech but effective chats or messages with people you like, and who like you.

This is why I asked everyone who agreed to go on to my contact list if they'd be willing to do one easy, single thing to get me elected. (Note: there's a lot of power in using the word 'willing' when you ask people for things. Rather than saying 'can you' or 'would you', 'are you willing?' makes people pause and feel like they're making a more meaningful choice. I reckon it makes them more likely to act. I use willing a lot.)

I asked: 'At election time, would you be willing to ask some of your friends to vote for me? I only need 1,337 votes. You probably have

"Thank goodness you're here!"

several hundred Facebook friends. You and five of your friends, asking their friends, could get me elected.'

Of course, not all of their Facebook friends would have been eligible to vote, but they could do the maths to realise they had more power and influence than they thought.

Most of us ignore advertising but accept messages and calls from family and friends.

Spend time writing the message that'll go out so it sounds friendly and is only making a small request – e.g. 'If you'd be willing to ask just five of your friends to vote for <Candidate X>, this could get them elected. Of course, if you have time to ask more people, that would be amazing.'

Modern technology makes it easy for people to instantly send the same message to all their contacts. Some might also post on social media, further expanding your reach, though social media posts are easily ignored and might not be seen in time.

Schedule time at the end of your campaign to contact everyone on your contact list

The end of my campaign was the most important bit. I considered it my last big-ditch effort and a way to reach people who'd likely never heard of me.

When voting time rolled around, I phoned or personally messaged 'my people' to remind them of what I wanted them to do, and to thank them in advance. Then I emailed, texted or instant messaged them a friendly, personal-sounding message they could cut and paste (yes, I see the irony in this) and asked them to send it to as many people as they were willing to.

The message they sent asked each recipient if they'd do the same and forward the message to their contacts.

This was old school viral messaging: spreading a message quickly to people who'd never met me, but who trusted their friends, who trusted me.

Get personal

This is the secret weapon you've been waiting to hear about – everyone wants the secret that will get them to the results they want, with little effort, so I'm about to tell you what that is. Ready?

Talk to as many people as personally as possible.

I talked about this back in the section Chapter 3: Reaching your people. You might like to whip back there for a refresher.

If you get invitations to talk to small groups or to go to people's houses, definitely accept them. Yes, you might feel nervous. But personal conversations are a million times better than other ways of trying to reach people and, guaranteed, you'll learn things you'd never otherwise hear about.

Talking to humans takes up time. However, it's the most valuable time you'll spend because all those people know other people. If they like you, they'll talk about you and they'll be willing to pass things on to their friends.

The absolute best thing about all this is that you'll be making genuine connections with people that'll potentially last the rest of your life. You're amplifying your own friendships and colouring in your sense of place.

People who help with your campaign will feel like they're part of something bigger than themselves. Your campaign might start a groundswell where people feel like they can have a say in politics.

Imagine that! A democracy where people actually participated willingly. This idea would terrify some politicians who'd prefer we shut up and consumed quietly.

Find any excuse to send a personal letter or note

When I say a personal letter or note, I mean a handwritten one. Using a pen. On paper.

If you want to invite someone to an event or say thank you for a conversation or for their help, a handwritten note will make the recipient feel really special. It doesn't matter if you write a short message or your handwriting is scrappy. Notes are worth their weight in gold.

If you've got a helper, get them to prepare envelopes and stamps (or pre-stamped ones to save time) – having the envelopes addressed for you is a big help when it comes to sitting down to write. Get them to add one of your business cards to each envelope and perhaps fold a blank page into the envelope ready for you to write on it. This is a great way for kids to help you with your campaign. Maybe not the envelope addressing bit, unless their handwriting is better than yours.

Carry these envelopes around with you and use five- or ten-minute gaps in your day to write notes to people. Then update your contact list to say you've done this. It's satisfying to watch it grow.

You'll be amazed at how many times you'll look at your list and see that you haven't contacted someone for a while. Pick up the phone to them or send a text or a DM on Facebook, and they'll respond with enthusiasm.

People are interested. But you need to be more interested in them. If they're keen to help, give them a specific task. Then thank them for it.

Events – the low-stress method

Invite people along to things you're planning to do anyway and call them events.

For example, if you go to the farmers market or some other event regularly, call it an 'event' and invite people to meet you there at a particular time and place, then be there. Call it a Listening Post or Chat 'n Chomp. Events sound so much more official if they have a name. Create a monthly Walk and Talk event at a local reserve. Be at the dog park every Monday afternoon. If your events show the kinds of things you care about, then they'll be effective promotional tools.

And sure, people might not turn up. If you're an introvert you might be relieved about that. It doesn't matter if it's something you were going to do anyway. You didn't waste any time. No-one needs to know that you hung out on your own at the farmers market or dog park for an hour. Anyone seeing your advertised event will assume that you had an event, they could have come if they wanted to, and they'll think that you're a confident event-haver. They'll remember your name and the kinds of things you like to do, which is the aim of your whole campaign.

You can encourage your supporters to organise events for you. Make them low-key, if you want.

I made an event called Watch, Think and Drink, based on going along to watch council meetings, then going to chat and have a drink afterwards. I'd been planning to attend meetings regularly as part of my campaign preparation and I realised that other people probably felt as intimidated about attending meetings as I had initially.

The Hobart Town Hall building is pretty olde worlde and imposing. I remember the first meeting I went to. The council chamber was unwelcoming. As a member of the public, I couldn't find the information the councillors were discussing in the hard copy agenda I picked up from the hallway. I didn't understand how the meeting was run. One of the councillors was ignoring the meeting and reading his professional journals on his laptop. Another was looking at his phone the whole time. Another threw a tantrum – a real one with shouting and foot stamping and leaving the room. It turns out that was something he did habitually, so after I saw this a few times, I started referring to it as a 'mantrum'.

Watch, Think and Drink wasn't a huge success but I did have a few hardy souls come along, watch the mantrums and other disappointing behaviour in shocked dismay, then join me for a drink.

"Thank goodness you're here!"

Your campaign will be a lot more fun if you go to events you like. Go to many more things than you usually would. Encourage your friends to invite you to things they care about. That's a low-stress way of meeting new people who are probably as nice as your friends.

You'll notice some of your competitors turning up at everything and taking photos with other people and their events as backdrops. Try not to use other people as a sideshow. If you go to events, think about how the event or organisation relates to your interests and take photos you can write something interesting about. Get permission to tag people or their organisation in your posts. Follow them on your social media.

It's OK to get photos of you at events, just don't make every single picture on your blog or social media feed one of you in an identical pose, in front of miscellaneous events.

People learn a lot about you when they see the things you support and promote. Try to show something of yourself and your interests and don't worry about looking perfect all the time. If people see your human side now you won't be worried about maintaining a perfect façade all the time later.

Public speaking

You won't actually die from public speaking, even if your body and brain tell you that you might. They're trying to save you from social death. And while you might never feel comfortable about speaking to groups, you can still get better at it.

Get some training or enlist an experienced friend to coach you.

"Thank goodness you're here!"

My tips:

- Smile as much as you can from the time you arrive, make small talk with the organisers and find ways to make yourself laugh. It relaxes you. It'll also make other candidates intimidated by how comfortable you look, because, trust me, everyone will be feeling stressed. Except for the sociopaths.

- When you stand up to speak, smile a slow smile and look around the room, making eye contact. If this freaks you out, get your friends or family to sit in the front row and let your eyes return to them as a kind of safe home base.

- Allow a moment of silence before you start talking. It's a power move. It also makes people stop chatting and listen.

- Tell a personal story first – 'When I first moved here I …' or 'My dog has always loved the local dog park but gets nervous about the number of e-scooter riders wearing business suits who go through there now …'. That being said, don't get too personal, and tell them about that mystery rash you had after visiting the Gold Coast. Make sure your story leads into whatever you're talking about. Your story should say: 'I'm someone just like you,' to people in the audience.

- If the idea of coming up with a personal story stresses you out, people will love you for launching right in: 'I'm Jo Blow and I want to make sure that all chicken fanciers feel included in the West Side Chicken Fancier Club!'

- Talk about positive things and opportunities – what you can do if elected, what you'd like to see etc – that way, if other candidates talk about scary, negative or frankly ludicrously aspirational things, you'll look like a better option, a practical, can-do person.

- Take a public speaking class. At the very least this will help you to meet a whole new group of people who you can practise talking to about your campaign.

- Alternatively: take an acting class, get a voice coach or take improv or stand-up comedy classes.

"Thank goodness you're here!"

→ **Stick to time!**

At speaking events or candidate's forums you must time yourself beforehand. If you're not a professional speaker then you Will Not Know What Five Minutes Feels Like. Running over time makes you look like an unprepared and/or selfish dummy. It also throws out the timing for the whole event.

Google how many words you can speak in two, five or ten minutes – however much time you're allocated. If you're including jokes that you hope people will laugh at, you'll need to cut down your word count even more. You need to leave time for people to laugh.

Turning up with five pages of closely written text for a five minute speech is amateur hour and the audience will sink down in their seats and Die Inside when you pull out your notes. I've watched speakers at a meet-the-candidates evening get cut off while they were still blah-ing through their introduction. They completely wasted their opportunity and actively turned people off them. That made me quite happy, actually, though I was sorry for the audience.

If you get elected, you'll have to work to rules and time limits. You're going to have to speak. It's a skill. Start getting better at it. You might never feel amazing at it – I still don't – but you'll get better every time you do it.

Doorknocking and why you might not need to do it

I decided not to do any doorknocking. You'll definitely get a lot of armchair experts telling you that you have to knock on doors if you want to get elected for anything.

Doorknocking has its place. If you're standing for a state or federal election and can get a team of people together to cover a whole suburb and ask questions and talk about you, and they're well trained, then that's potentially useful. But it's a big logistical exercise.

"Thank goodness you're here!"

96

I have been involved in doorknocking for those kinds of large campaigns, so I have a fair grasp on how many doors you can knock on in an hour and how people respond. It's cold-calling.

Do your own sums.

I can knock on about 12 doors an hour. On a very good day, maybe 7 people might answer, four will say 'not interested,' two will be friendly and open to talking briefly, one will talk for way too long about an unrelated subject …

It was a far better use of my time, and less nerve-wracking, to go to events that interested me and have warm, personal conversations with like-minded people who were open to chatting. So long as I made sure to actually talk to lots of people, rather than chickening out and just talking to one, I'd find great new supporters, give them my postcard to pass along to their friends and get their details on my contact list.

I also got wine. And often cheese.
This is my opinion. Do your own sums.

Think of alternatives to doorknocking that feel good to you. How can you talk to people in your area? Where do they go? Take your dog, or borrow a dog, and go where people are – a dog exercise area. Hang around at the local pub or café. Talk to the people who talk to everyone – your butcher, hairdresser, newsagent …

Email newsletters

I chose to do an e-newsletter after a lot of dickering. I write for a living, so I know they take a lot of time and effort to write and edit.

I called people from my contact list to ask if I could add them to my mailing list, assuring them that they could easily unsubscribe. Then I set up an online account and started sending them chatty, personal messages and inviting them to events. This was a good way to reach people who don't enjoy using social media. They also found it easy to respond to me by hitting Reply. Some people forwarded my emails to friends, who then signed up to receive them. It was encouraging to talk with people this way and find out what they were thinking about.

If you do write an e-newsletter, create a template that has all your contact information somewhere on it, along with any other info you're legally required to provide (according to the rules of your election).

Make a plan for your e-newsletters so they go out at key times and get all your key messages across.

I planned and drafted my e-newsletters starting from the last one I planned to send (announcing the results of the election count) through to the first one about my campaign launch.

Your plan might look something like this, working back from the end to the beginning of your campaign:

- The results are in (I got in! or I didn't get in but I loved having your support).

- Thank you for voting, now we wait.

- It's time to vote – please vote for me and ask your friends and family to vote.

- One-week reminder: e.g. in only a week you'll be able to vote.

- Mid-campaign message(s).

- Campaign launch message (potentially modify this one so people who join your mailing list later receive this as a welcome email explaining what you're all about).

Your e-newsletter should explicitly ask for votes, and encourage your readers to talk to their co-workers, friends and families about you. Tell them how many votes you need. Ask them to forward your e-newsletter to five people and to ask their five people to pass it along to five others.

Letterboxing – and other, better ways to get your campaign information into the world

If you read the section in Chapter 4: Flyers or brochures you'll know my opinion on mass-produced pieces of paper that have a picture of your head and Vote 1 on them. Straight into the recycling bin is where those will go.

If you can, put your flyers or postcards into people's hands

Think about packaging your flyers to give a relatively small number to anyone who supports you. Every time someone's encouraging about your campaign, ask them if they know 5 or 7 or even 10 people who might vote for you, then give them this number of flyers and they'll be more likely to hand them out. See Chapter 7: Anatomy of my campaign for an example of how I packaged mine.

If the person taking your flyers says, 'I'll put them in the tea room at work,' I'd encourage you to say, 'I'd rather you give them to people in person – that'll make them much more likely to vote for me. If you just leave them around, people won't pick them up.'

Things left around in piles with other things in piles might, just might, get picked up and read, but in all likelihood they'll be ignored.

Make sure that your supporters know the power of their personal recommendations. Each of us has more power to influence than we know. Even if we influence just a few people, the knock-on effect can be significant.

You might end up with super-supporters who come back time and time again to collect and distribute more of your flyers. If you make them attractive or humorous, then they're much more shareable.

Ideally, a keep-able flyer or brochure being put into someone's hand by a person they trust, who is telling your story, is going to be much

"Thank goodness you're here!"

more influential than sliding it into someone's slug-filled letterbox alongside some ads for pizza and gutter cleaning.

Sending things in the post

If you're aiming to make all your contacts with people as personal as possible, consider posting or hand-delivering information to people on your list of contacts. Bear in mind that it takes time to print or handwrite and deliver things by hand. Postage is expensive too, so make it count.

I sent a lot of handwritten notes (something I do in my normal life, not just when campaigning) because people love getting real mail in their letterbox. I wrote to people to continue conversations and send articles or clippings, to say thank you, or to invite them to small events.

Make sure you have people's permission to send them things by mail. Well, you don't strictly need their permission, but I reckon you should make sure they won't be creeped out by you knowing their address.

How do you do non-creepy posting? When you're collecting people's contact info during your campaigning, ask if you can pop something in their post box every now and then. If they don't give you an enthusiastic yes, then don't do it.

If you're an introvert, just post things to your close friends.

They'll love it. Maybe enclose a couple of copies of your campaign material and ask if they'd like to give them to their friends.

Put stuff into letterboxes

If you're determined to get your well-designed, beautiful and/or informative flyers or postcards into letterboxes across your neighbourhood, then you can either pay a distribution company to deliver them, do it yourself, or invite some volunteers to help you.

I've talked a lot about what should go on to a flyer to make it effective, in Chapter 4: Flyers or brochures.

If you're lucky enough to have volunteers, maybe get one of them to take on the job of printing maps of locations to deliver to, compiling the correct number of flyers to go with each map, and making sure everything is delivered on time.

Signs and posters

In Chapter 4: Signs and posters I encouraged you to work out the rules that apply to signs and posters for your kind of election and to plan for getting them printed, picked up, put up, maintained, taken down and stored or disposed of.

If you can find someone to project manage all your signs and posters, that'll free you up considerably. Otherwise, plan all the locations you need to visit, strap on your tool belt and get out there. You'll need a vehicle that can carry your signs and tools, wooden or metal stakes, drills with spare batteries, screws, wire, cable ties, hammers and an info sheet containing your contact details to leave with property owners. Signs often get defaced or broken, so you'll want to be able to replace them quickly.

Schedule extra time to talk to anyone who's kind enough to let you erect a sign. Add them to your contact database. Offer them your flyers etc so they can tell people your story. If they're willing to support you publicly by hosting your sign or poster, they'll presumably be happy to ask their friends and family to vote for you.

"Thank goodness you're here!"

Give them all the info they need to spread the word.

This is why having a team of sign-/poster-erectors can be helpful –
you're the candidate, so you should be available to talk to anyone
and everyone, every chance you get. If you have a mouth full of nails
(don't hold nails in your mouth) you can't talk.

Give your sign and poster team lots of love. It's a hard job and can
feel pretty thankless.

Don't forget to schedule time to take down signs and posters at the
end of a campaign. Make room in your shed to store them, offer
them to friends to use as tree-guards, or plan to dispose of them.

Getting traditional media

You might feel Ughhh at the thought of trying to get yourself into your
local paper, on TV or radio. There are definitely some kinds of people
who love getting their names out there in public, and they don't care
how they do it.

If you're not that person, please don't discount it entirely.

Think about it: media organisations need stories. It's hard work to
find enough stories to fill all their websites, radio time or newspaper
space, so they often accept whatever is sent to them, if it's
presented in a way they can easily use.

Your local talk-back radio station has many hours of empty time to
fill. They need people to interview. What do you have to talk about
that might interest them? Think about your points of difference. Are
you a candidate who can talk about a visible or invisible disability?
Do you have a background in wastewater treatment and want to see
your local streams cleaned up? As someone from a cultural minority
group, do you have ideas about how to increase all the benefits of
welcoming different kinds of people into the community? As the
carer of a super-sporty child, do you have ideas for local parent–
teacher groups to share local resources?

If you pitch interesting stories to media organisations, they'll
remember you as a reliable source for information on these topics

and they'll potentially call you for comments on related stories. Make a relationship with the people who manage the columns, online sites, radio shows or TV segments, and let them know all the things you're happy to talk to them about.

This is how people get radio time. If you find yourself tuned into your local radio station saying, 'Why the heck do they keep interviewing that dweeb?' be aware that, sure, that person might be a dweeb, but they're a dweeb who offered to be interviewed. They're available. They show up when contacted. They probably call up and offer to speak.

One great way to get dweebs off the radio or out of the paper is to get yourself in there. Encourage other people who're doing great stuff to get in there too.

You don't need to use the media. If you think you can reach enough voters by other means, then stick with your plan. But don't completely write it off. It's a good way to reach lots of people, particularly when you're using local media.

Every media person you meet is also a potential voter.

→ **How to prepare for being interviewed by local media**

Talk to the journalist or the person managing the segment or show. Ask how the interview will work. How much time will you have? Can you phone in or do you need to come to the station or meet a journalist somewhere?

Know your key points. Send a summary beforehand, take a copy to give the interviewer on the day and keep a copy for yourself.

Gird your loins so you're ready to make your key points in the time available. If it looks like the interviewer isn't going to give you a chance to say what you want, you'll need to plough on and say what you need to say: 'Before I go, I'd love people to know that I'm standing for election to the Swan-Fanciers Association this March so we can save these magnificent birds. I'd love your vote.'

"Thank goodness you're here!"

During the interview, pretend you're talking to someone you really like. Imagine your best friend has appeared right over the interviewer's shoulder and talk to them. This will brighten up your voice and make you look and sound genuinely happy.

For TV, don't wear stripes and don't wear green if there's any possibility you'll be in front of a green screen (where they project different backgrounds).

For radio, they might also film your interview for their website, so you'll need to make sure you still look presentable. Weird, right?

Don't forget that everyone you meet, including reporters and radio station staff, could be a potential voter (depending on your type of election), so be lovely to everyone. Do that everywhere you go.

How do you get ideas for writing posts, articles or podcast episodes?

Collect ideas and take photos so your e-news or social media posts are interesting

If you decide to use social media, regardless of the platform you'll need things to talk about so you can post regularly. It's a pain to find yourself without ideas.

Plan ahead and capture a stack of ideas you can go to for an easy discussion point when you need one.

Keep a bunch of pages free in your notebook so you can note down topics to write about. This is your go-to list when you run out of ideas for your e-newsletter or social media posts.

Look online for ideas and bookmark them, then add them to your go-to list for when you're low on inspiration. If you link to community groups or research on topics that interest you, and say a bit about why you're sharing them, that not only shows people what's

"Thank goodness you're here!"

important to you, it includes them in a conversation.

I kept my post ideas on an Excel spreadsheet and I noted when I'd used each idea. Many ideas can be broken down into smaller ideas and spread out to match the phases of your campaign, as discussed in Chapter 4: Making a plan. You can also repeat the same idea with slightly different wording in different places, e.g. on your blog, in your e-newsletter, on social media etc.

I scheduled a lot of blog and social media posts ahead of time because some were quick and some required a lot more time to think about and write. Scheduling easy ones gave me some breathing room and allowed me to publish a consistent stream of messages, which kept me motivated and gave me time to write longer pieces that needed more research.

Creative ideas to reach more people, with minimal effort

How do you reach the people who might vote for you? I've talked about the typical election-y things above. Now think creatively. Your aim is to meet new, like-minded people, hear their points of view, let them know you're standing for election, collect their contact details and ask for their vote.

get a handy template

Aside from joining and promoting all the groups you know who share your values, which we already covered in Chapter 5: Events – the low-stress method, you need to meet a range of people.

Here are my ideas for low-effort, high-return, zero-waste events and promotions:

Make social media easier with regular posts that show your human side: What do you enjoy looking at? Create a regular post with photos you take and stockpile while you're out and about, preferably of something that relates to your town or your interests. For example, you might schedule an easy post each Wednesday featuring a post of a photo of a letterbox, bicycle, cloud, book, shoe, dog, paving stone, native animal or plant – whatever you're interested in.

Encourage other people to tag you in if they take photos of you. And invite them to share their own photos. If it catches on, people will enjoy your more human side when they see your 'Letterbox Thursday,' 'Dog Wednesday' or 'Public Transport Friday' posts each week.

BBQ, afternoon tea: sometimes called a kitchen cabinet meeting. Get a friend to invite their friends to meet you over a cup of tea or snacks. Spend some time meeting new people in a relaxed setting. Ask them what they think about a particular subject that's on everyone's mind where you live.

Clothing swap: get someone to organise a clothes swap. I went to an incredible one at someone's house and spent the afternoon with a whole bunch of women drinking champagne, laughing and trying on clothes.

Tool swap, bike swap, or appliance swap: this is like a clothing swap, but you'll likely keep your gear on.

Walk and talk session: organise to meet somewhere and go for a walk so people can tell you about their neighbourhood or discuss a particular topic you want their views about.

Dog park loitering: go and sit at a dog park and someone will invariably come and sit and talk to you.

Become a regular at a local café or pub: get to know the staff somewhere. Have lots of your meetings there. This will give you a secure home base and allow a few people to get to know you well. Pub and café staff have big networks, so if they vouch for you, that can mean a lot.

Organise a showing of a documentary that means a lot to you, followed by a discussion.

Print t-shirts or bags, preferably using pre-loved items so people can get hands-on and make their own materials to support you. Creating branded campaign t-shirts onto shirts people already own can be a lot of fun. Crafting- or making-type events are fun and relaxing and give people time to talk and listen while their hands are busy.

Make a folding screen to put inside your car windscreen and rear window when it's parked. You could make one from cardboard or overlay a durable paper one on a commercial folding sun reflector, advertising your campaign. Other people might be willing to also put these into their cars and park them in prominent positions. (You might need permission to do this in some places, for some kinds of campaigns.)

Regularly attend a local market for a series of months during your campaign and get permission to set up a Listening Booth. Or do it unofficially by advertising on social media that you'll be at a particular place each week or month, if they want to come and talk. Organise for your friends to come so you're not lonesome if no-one else turns up. An added bonus is you'll get to know the market organisers and other stallholders, who probably know everyone.

Make a custom coat for your dog that advertises your campaign in a lighthearted way.

Custom-make a sign you can hang on your bike when it's locked up around town. If your election platform is a bit contentious, be careful about whether this might invite someone to damage it.

Can't think of your own ideas? Ask a creative friend to help you to brainstorm easy events that don't require you to organise venues or collect RSVPs – and that you'll have fun attending even if no-one else comes.

"Thank goodness you're here!"

Chapter 6

Decided this whole getting-elected idea isn't for you? Keep reading, you can still change things

Not for you? That's understandable

You might have decided that the whole idea of campaigning and selling yourself and talking to strangers makes you want to crawl into the cupboard and die – I hear you loud and clear. That's how I felt a lot of the time while I was doing it.

I did get elected, and, even though I'd done my homework on what the job would be like, I resigned before finishing my full term. My main reason was the effect it had on my ability to work as a single, self-employed person while doing a full-time-with-overtime public role.

If you've read this far and are thinking, 'I don't want to do this,' then that's good and fine.

It's better to be honest with yourself if you don't have the time, resources or energy to do it, or you do want to do it but now's not a good time.

Standing for election is only one way to be a part of the decisions that are made where you live. You might find you can be far more effective in creating change in other ways.

Support someone else to run

If you decide not to run for election, you can still change your town, city or organisation by helping one of the other candidates with their campaign.

Is there a candidate you admire or who you wonder about? Get in touch with them. Phone them up and meet them for coffee. I can tell you now: campaigning is extremely lonely. Having an actual human get in touch is an immense confidence boost and often leads to interesting connections.

If they're a plonker, you'll know more about them and it'll help you decide whether to vote for them yourself. If they look really good but their campaign is a bit iffy, why not share some ideas from this book? You could be the one to help them with their contact list or mail-outs

"Thank goodness you're here!"

or scheduling social media posts or by talking them up. You could write letters to the paper about them and the subjects that interest them. You could help them to identify groups and organisations that they could visit or join. You could share their posts on social media and hand out their information.

There are a million ways you could help someone. In fact, I bet you'd come up with far more ways to help someone else than you would for your own campaign. We humans are a bit weird like that.

The biggest way you can help someone's campaign is to ask your friends to vote for them and to spread good news stories about them that are easily repeatable:

> 'Armin is interested in public health and preserving our environment. He was a teacher for 20 years.'

> 'Ji-Woo is a cellist who's keen on community gardens and transport. She loves cycling.'

> 'Emma is terrific – very professional and energetic and able to get along with everyone. She also has a cocker spaniel named Garibald.'

Be an opinion-shaper and influence voters in coming elections

You could be the opinion-shaper in your group of friends.

If you're good at research and enjoy coming up with ways to measure things, you could work out the criteria you'll use to compare candidates against. Then you could distribute that to your friends so they can start thinking more critically.

Here's my personal How to Vote criteria I use when short-listing candidates for all the elections I have the good fortune to vote in:

- Does this person seem to understand the role they'll be doing if elected?
- How do they seem to make decisions? (Essential: since I'll be voting for them to make decisions on my behalf, I want to know

they have a good framework for making future decisions, based on more than gut instinct or robust self-confidence.)

- Do they talk about research and subject-matter experts or make sweeping or emotive statements?

- When I google them do I find:

  o They have some kind of up-to-date online presence? It's rare for people not to, especially if they're standing for a prominent position.

  o They've been in the paper for mistreating people or animals or misusing power or money? (Note: if they're alleged to have done something dodgy but not been found guilty, I give them the benefit of the doubt and delve a little more deeply.)

- Will they add a new perspective to the organisation they'll be joining?

Then I'll go old-school and ask around. My city is small. People know people who are usually happy to tell you what someone's like to work with or what they're really good (or bad) at. Take this all with a grain of salt but do pay attention if similar types of stories come up repeatedly.

Work with a decision-maker who's already doing a good job

You'd be amazed – as I am constantly amazed – at what a single contact with the right person can achieve. You could get what you want to happen, without getting elected yourself.

- Are you interested in the built environment – what gets put up, knocked down or changed?

- Do you want the board you're interested in joining to only invest in ethical companies?

- Can you see opportunities for your school's student representative group to join a coalition with other schools?

- Could your local men's shed benefit from including different kinds of people you have links with?

- Do you want more or different events in the community?

- Are you concerned about bushfires or droughts or flooding rains?

Find a friendly representative – heck, email all of them and see who bothers to answer. Then see if you can meet them or talk on the phone. Seriously, not many people ask to do this. You will be amazed at how a polite and personable conversation can bump your issue way up on their list of things to think about.

Your rep will be more open to listening to your requests and suggestions once they know you. Send them a summary of your issues and the benefits of solving these. Add links to reputable sources they can go to for more information. Throw in some pictures or graphs to illustrate your points. If they understand what you're talking about, and see its importance, they'll be far more likely to champion your issue. You can be a valuable resource for them by bringing them well-researched information they can act on.

Great representatives can do so much more when they're supported by excellent people like you.

Chapter 7

Anatomy of my campaign

"Thank goodness you're here!"

What: Hobart City Council election (now called City of Hobart)

Where: Hobart, the capital city of the state of Tasmania, Australia

When: 2014

Budget: A$2,500 (of which, $1,426 was donated) plus around a year of my time. I did my own graphic design.

How many positions were being filled: 12

How many candidates ran in this election: 30

How many candidates were standing for re-election: 12

How long had some councillors served on the council already: possibly longer than you've been alive

How many #1 votes I thought I needed: 1,337

How many votes I was elected with: 704 #1 votes. This means I was elected by people numbering me #2, #3 or #4 on their voting forms in our state's proportional representation system.

And, to demonstrate the power of getting people to follow through and vote: 37,624 voters were enrolled to vote in this election – only 18,993 actually voted (about half). Of those who voted, 1,418 stuffed up their ballot papers, so those weren't counted. Some councillors were elected with only 400 votes. You probably have close to 400 friends following your social media accounts. Isn't it mind-blowing to think that you and your friends could decide an election? Your individual votes can make a huge collective difference.

My bottom-line ethical decisions

I decided that my campaign was going to focus on positive things, without being airy-fairy. I didn't lie, cheat, pull other people down, try to make folks feel fearful or pretend to like people or things.

My values and motivations

I was disappointed in the kinds of people who were the elected decision-makers in the city I love, and the kinds of decisions they were making. I wanted to see people in those roles behaving ethically and professionally, paying attention, making reasoned decisions, really listening and trying to do things the community clearly said they wanted.

I wanted to show residents in my town, who were feeling burned out and cynical about politics, that they should and could expect different kinds of representatives. I also wanted to show non-voters that their decision not to vote resulted in truly disappointing people getting elected with a paltry number of votes.

The 'voice' I used in my campaign was personal, humorous, plain speaking, realistic but positive (not using 'typical politician' sneer and smear techniques).

Challenges

These were the challenges I faced in my council election.

- Voting for council elections in Tasmania isn't compulsory.
- The people I thought might share my values were aged 35–50, and people in this age group tend not to vote in council elections.
- Young adults aged 18+ (Australian voting age) might not have enrolled to vote, so I risked missing out on votes from young people who'd like to influence the future of their city.
- I wasn't well known in my community.

"Thank goodness you're here!"

- Many of the standing members had/still have (as I write this) been in their jobs longer than lots of us have been alive – their name recognition was strong, even when that recognition, in some cases, has resulted from dubious behaviour.

- Voting is done by postal ballot – yes, it arrives in the post. There are two voting forms and they have to be filled in correctly and posted back.

- People have several weeks to vote – that's a lot of time for someone to mean to vote and then forget.

- The voting instructions aren't foolproof and require reasonable comprehension and focus – a surprising number of invalid votes are received at each election.

- Oh, and not many people know what councils or councillors actually do and think the whole thing is too boring to contemplate.

My campaign aimed at getting over all these potential hurdles. I addressed each of these challenges every single chance I got throughout my campaign.

My campaign activities

I decided early in the piece what I was and wasn't going to do. This sometimes came down to a matter of what was a good use of my time and effort, what I thought would appeal to my potential voters, and what felt comfortable.

Things I decided to do: talk to people in person, make phone calls, send personal emails, send personal direct messages via social media, give people humorous postcards or other campaign materials that weren't too highly branded, that they might keep and display and they'd be happy to hand on to their friends and family.

Things I decided not to do: doorknocking, yard signs, pay for newspaper ads or write letters to the paper.

Part-way through the campaign I decided to buy an electric scooter (as in a Vespa-type scooter that uses an electric battery rather than petrol) and have it sign-written as a kind of moving campaign ad. It was also a cheap, handy way to get around.

I created a 'secret' poster of a love poem I'd written to Hobart. This was my version of a campaign poster, since I wasn't keen to put pictures of my head onto signs in front yards all over town. I gave the posters to people on the condition that they kept them private. It turns out that people love private things so much that they tell their friends about them. The secret posters became so popular I spent a lot of time printing and giving them out. There's more on this in the section below about my campaign materials.

Main steps in my campaign

I did things that felt comfortable to me and that I thought would appeal to the people who might vote for me.

- I went and watched some council meetings and thought hard about the whole situation I might be getting myself into if elected.

- I attended meetings with my mentor, who explained what was happening, who was who, and told me amusing but terrible stories about how long it took the council to finally concede that female reps weren't going away, and get around to putting in a ladies loo. Just one, though. Little did they realise that, ahem, a trickle would become a flood when it came to more diverse representation.

- I talked to people who'd worked for the council and been on councils in other towns and states.

- I did some homework to make sure I was eligible and to find out the critical dates and rules. I filed all this info in folders on my computer and marked important dates on my calendar.

- I looked at past candidate statements and the photos they'd used, so I could decide what worked and what didn't. I wrote a rough draft of my candidate statement.

- I made a plan – working out my main motivation and the kinds of people I thought would care about the things I cared about. Then I broke my campaign into phases to fit the time available, and wrote draft messages to fit each phase (I've summarised these in the next section).

- I dumped all of my contacts from my phone and computer into a spreadsheet to see how many likely votes I could get, and how many extra people I'd need to reach.

- I talked to people about my plan and ran my ideas past them. I listened to what they said and the questions they asked and revised my messages.

- I worked out every possible barrier someone might have to voting for me and planned ways to address these. I built those in to my messages.

- I wrote and re-wrote what I thought was a persuasive candidate statement and chose the photo I used throughout my campaign and on the candidate statement that would go out in the post to voters.

- I drafted all kinds of flyers, postcards and business cards, planned social media posts and e-newsletter content and scheduled these into the major phases of my campaign.

- I used my contact list to get in touch with enough people who might know enough people who'd vote for me – and encouraged them to vote (for anyone), telling them how few votes were required to elect new representatives if they didn't like the ones they had.

- I focused the first part of my campaign on getting eligible people to register to vote – especially parents of young people who'd have turned 18 in the past year, so they could encourage them to get on the electoral roll.

- I asked everyone I spoke with to vote for me – giving them postcards to pass along to friends, if they were willing to do that. If they said they were voting for someone else, I asked them for their #2 or #3 preference votes, in line with our state's electoral system.

- I collected the contact details of anyone who was vaguely positive about my campaign, promising not to spam them, and I added them to my contacts list and e-newsletter list.

- I explained to absolutely anyone who'd listen that it was a postal vote, told them the date the voting forms would arrive in the mail, and that they'd need to fill in their form and post it back. I included a picture of a typical Australia Post post box on most of my campaign material as a visual reminder.

- Just before the election period started, I spent considerable time getting in touch in person to remind 'my people' to vote, and to ask them to ask their family and friends to vote. I did this by phoning and sending texts, emails, direct messages or notes in the post. I even sent them suggested wording they could forward in a text message or email to their friends and family, introducing me, asking for their vote, explaining that it was a postal vote and telling them how to vote correctly.

- I gave them another reminder before the two-week voting period ended.

My campaign phases and messages

These were my messages for the major phases of my campaign.

1. 'I'm planning to stand for election.'

   a. If they didn't know about the election or what council does, I told them in person, added them to my contacts list and sent a follow-up email about it. This email encouraged them to check to see whether they, and anyone else in their household, was enrolled to vote.

2. 'Your vote is powerful.'

   a. Help people to understand how few votes are required to elect a representative, so they understand how powerful their vote can be.

   b. Ask if they or their young people are enrolled to vote and, if not, encourage them to sign up soon.

   c. If they were business owners, encourage them to sign up to the General Manager's list to be eligible for an additional vote. Yes, where I live, people who know the rules and fit the rules can vote more than once.

3. 'If you don't vote, then other people will and they'll get the representatives they want, who might not be what you, or the city, needs.'

4. 'Voting will happen on this date. The voting form will arrive in the post and you've got to fill it in and post it back before the closing date.'

5. 'Please vote for me and ask your friends and family to vote for me.'

   a. Carefully wrote a friendly, clear message to send to people after the voting forms had been posted out to households, asking for their vote.

   b. When they responded, I thanked them and asked if they'd be willing to ask their family and friends to vote for me. If yes, I forwarded them another carefully written text explaining exactly how to vote for me, so they could forward this on.

6. 'Thank you. Here are the polling results. Here's what'll happen next. Keep voting every chance you get in future.'

Media

I only sent out a few media releases, but I probably should have sent more. It was hard to keep myself motivated and I found the idea of pitching myself to the media extremely uncomfortable.

I did get some media – I think I was in three newspaper stories with photographs.

One story featured my electric scooter – so, as I said, think carefully about gimmicks. If you're going to use one, make sure it fits with your values, reinforces your message, helps you in some way and even makes you smile. In this case, it helped me to get around too.

The main reason I got media without pursuing it vigorously was that I decided part-way through my campaign to stand for the position of mayor – in for a penny and all that. I didn't think I'd actually get elected as mayor, since the other candidates had much higher profiles and also some experience of doing that job. I had a rush of blood and thought, why not?

It was a gamble. On the one hand, standing for the position of mayor got me more media exposure than I'd have received simply standing as a councillor (or 'alderman' as the position was then called), since our local paper generally does a story about the people running for mayor. It also garnered me an invitation to speak at a conservative local business group's breakfast.

On the other hand, it was an extra thing to have to explain to people who already weren't very interested in this election. Moreover, it meant voters effectively needed to vote for me twice, on two different forms: once for me to be a councillor and once for me to be mayor. If I didn't get enough votes to be elected as councillor I couldn't become mayor, even if I got enough votes for that position. There was a real risk people might give me a vote for mayor and ignore the other form, accidentally knocking me out.

My campaign materials

Graphic design

Knowing the importance of consistency, I picked a colour scheme for my campaign based on the headshot I decided to use during my campaign and in my candidate statement. I used the colour of my top, my lipstick and eyes. I definitely considered the implication of using colours people might associate with particular political parties, but it's pretty hard to avoid those colours completely.

I chose a clear, rounded font that I liked and used it consistently, including to write my initials and name on all my materials. I eventually had a 3D printed name badge made in this font.

Business cards

My campaign business cards were designed to be keep-able, to start promoting my name, branding and the photo that would be on my candidate statement. They were an invitation for people to come along on the 'adventure' of my campaign. The card was an opener, a conversation-starter.

I wrote the cards to encourage people to think about how much power they really have in everyday life, while using examples of the things I care about for the city. It was a way of focusing on their values while also talking about my own.

Having cards made me feel committed and confident (even when I was freaking out).

The back of the card certainly has a big, optimistic statement on it. 'Let's change the world – you and me.' When I'd give a card to someone I'd joke that, while we couldn't change the whole world, we could at least change this little part of the world we lived in, our city.

The post box graphic was important during the first phase of my campaign, to remind people that the election would be done by postal vote. Most people are still surprised when I tell them this, as all our other state and federal voting is done at a polling booth. That explains why relatively few people vote in council elections, I suppose – it's just not on their radar. By the way, 'HCC' stood for the Hobart City Council – it was a well-known acronym at the time.

Postcards with belly bands

People trust people they know. However, it can feel uncomfortable to bring up the subject of politics with your friends. I created these cards so my supporters could have something non-tacky and hopefully keep-able and shareable to hand to someone – while feeling good that they were helping me to get 10 votes. I figured that it'd feel possible to give away 10 cards. People were relieved I wasn't asking them to go doorknocking or putting leaflets into mailboxes.

I made two different 'flavours' of cards and wrapped them with a belly band, telling the recipient that they had the power to get me elected. The belly bands made them look special, like a gift. This was intended to be lighthearted and motivating.

Some of my supporters came back to get many more packs to distribute. In fact, some wonderful people were postcard super-spreaders.

EVERY ACT IS A VOTE.

You're subversive. Yes, you. You're subversive in the most wonderful way when you choose to contribute rather than complain, to seek to understand, to elect public leaders who put the civil back into the civic, and to speak up when others' rights are trodden on ... Every action is a vote for the sort of world you want. Vote, you good thing, you.

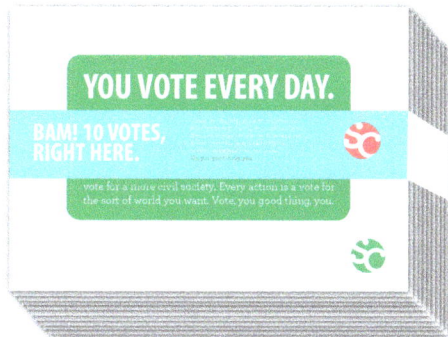

YOU VOTE EVERY DAY.

BAM! 10 VOTES, RIGHT HERE.

vote for a more civil society. Every action is a vote for the sort of world you want. Vote, you good thing, you.

Ten postcards, two of each type, wrapped with a belly band telling people they had the power to get me elected.

YOU VOTE EVERY DAY.

When you catch the bus you vote for buses to be there when you need them. When you vote for local jobs with fair cycle you vote for awesomeness. breath and speak kindly instead vote for a more civil society. Ever the sort of world you want. Vote.

VOTE FOR THE HOBART YOU WANT

I'll tell you what I want, what I really really want ...

I want Hobart to have more local businesses, rather than more chain stores. I hanker after a centralised transit zone, a promenade along the waterfront and suburbs that each have a unique personality.

I want us to combine our working, education, childcare and retirement spaces to regain a true sense of community - and I want us to live at human speed. If you want an alderman who's cheery, thoughtful, forthright and not a jerk, please consider voting for me this October.

I won't bore you.

Suzy Cooper .com.au
for Hobart City Council

• FB: www.facebook.com/SuzyCooperTasmania
• web: suzycooper.com.au
• 0439 933 374 • suzy@suzycooper.com.au
• PO Box 395 Lenah Valley TAS 7008

YOU VOTE EVERY DAY.
www.suzycooper.com.au

Bumper stickers

I found a local printer who could make small numbers of stickers for me. I went with the statement: 'you vote every day' to tie in to my campaign idea that many of your daily decisions are a kind of vote for the sort of world you want to live in, and your vote for council could make a significant change to your local community.

These stickers had my branding on them and were intended as a talking point for whoever had them on their car, so they'd talk about my campaign to anyone who asked.

Some people hate stickers. That's OK. I'm not really a sticker person myself. People who do like them are more likely to put them on their car or somewhere else if the stickers are attractive and either pithy or funny.

Yes, stickers are plastic. Plastic is bad.

Posters

OK, I wrote a love poem to my city. I didn't intend it to become public but I showed a friend who suggested I share it. I put the text over a silhouette of the mountain that stands behind my city, kunanyi / Mount Wellington, and showed it to someone else. They wanted one. Then their friend wanted one.

I printed them at A2 size on good-quality card, so they'd last. They had minimal branding, with my name on the bottom corner.

At one point near the end of my campaign I was busier making and distributing posters than anything else. This was a great opportunity to talk to people face-to-face and explain why I was standing and why I needed their votes. I added all these people to my mailing lists, asked them if I could send them a reminder at voting time and gave them packs of my postcards, so they could invite their friends to vote for me too. Talking to people in person was a big energy boost at a time when I was seriously questioning why I was doing this at all.

This goes to show that it's OK to do things that are heartfelt, even if you worry they're naff.

"Thank goodness you're here!"

Name tag

My name tag used the same font that I used for all my campaign brochures, and was made with a 3D printer. It's amazingly handy having your own name badge to put on when you go to events. And it's much nicer to re-use one than end up with a handwritten one or a tacky plastic one that'll get into waterways and choke whales. Yes, I know that 3D printers use plastic, but, since I'm still using that name tag seven years after my campaign, it's not a single-use jobbie.

Cinema ads

I advertised at my local art-house cinema because I thought that's where thinking left-leaning prospective voters go. At the time cinema advertising was relatively cheap and, as part of the deal, they'd let me put my flyers in the lobby. One of my donors gave me money to pay for my cinema ads, and I advertised over two months in the last third of my campaign.

My message was intended to make a statement about events at the time, whereby some people were trying to make money from beautiful natural places. But it was too oblique – probably self-indulgent, really. I was trying to share my values with a slightly cryptic statement hoping to generate enough curiosity that viewers would pick up my flyer.

It was a fizzer of an idea. Not many flyers got picked up.

I should have been more direct with my message. After all, when I go to the movies I'm not really looking at the ads. I'm trying to bite into my choc top without making a mess.

Invitations to events

I created events inviting people to come and watch a council meeting and then go for a drink with me afterwards to discuss what they'd seen. I called these Watch, Think and Drink.

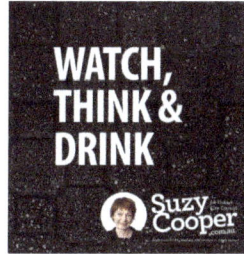

Scooter sign-writing

I bought an electric scooter partway through my campaign, because I wanted to replace my petrol scooter with an electric one. When I saw its lovely white panels, I had a rush of blood and decided to sign-write it. My graphic designer buddy suggested getting it wrapped and he helped to modify my designs to fit the panels and the big white storage box on the back (which I believe was a pizza delivery box and was extremely handy for carrying all my groceries).

Riding around with my name all over something was pretty embarrassing, but twice I found notes of encouragement stuck to it, one with a five dollar campaign donation. And that's not nothing.

It also got me an article in the local newspaper, which is a publication that likes gimmicks.

Even though I'd bought the scooter because it was a great non-fossil-fuel-using-car-alternative, I did realise that it still opened me up for criticism because the scooter itself had panels made of plastic, the sign-writing used plastic stickers, and electric vehicles have high embodied energy costs. I wasn't kidding myself that I was a saviour of the environment, but I did feel happy that it created fewer emissions than my petrol scooter. It was extremely convenient to get around on when I didn't want to walk, cycle or take the bus. Quite simply, it was a lot of fun during a time when I felt stressed on most days.

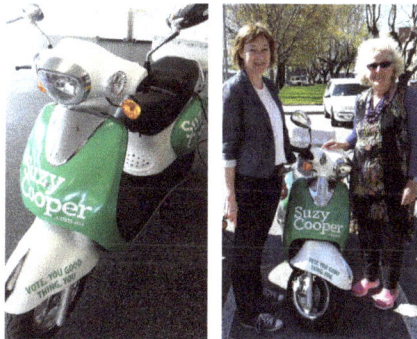

"Thank goodness you're here!"

I felt free, like I was flying on night-time rides on deserted Hobart streets as I silently swooped (with great care, don't worry, Dad) down vertiginous streets.

My candidate statement and photo

I decided that I wanted to look natural and approachable in my photo, and that it had to look good in black and white, since that's how it would appear with the candidate statement that went out with the voting forms.

I used a professional headshot I'd had taken when I was performing stand-up comedy.

Hobart is your city. This election, take your city back.

I'm a scientist and writer with a good head on my shoulders, a warm heart and pep in my step. Council decisions should include you. We have the tools, we need the will.

The Hobart I want will be known for its zest and life, its fairness, its unique local businesses, its remarkable creative people, its researchers and thinkers, its resourceful problem-solvers, its history and its future prospects, and its stunning natural surrounds. Let's make it so. Please vote for Suzy Cooper as Alderman and Lord Mayor (and ask your friends to vote, too).

Conclusion

Well, you've made it to the end of this book.

I hope it got you thinking about different ways you might be able to influence the decisions that are made in the place where you live, whether you decide to nominate for election, help someone else to get elected or support someone who's already in a role.

I bet you'll find lots of organisations in your area that need people to roll up their sleeves and help do the things they're set up to do. Join them. Take part in their events. Think about joining their committees.

Things can be different. You can make them different.

You change the world in tiny and maybe even enormous ways every time you listen carefully to people when they talk to you, when you introduce people who have similar interests, and when you apply your brain, your heart and your energy to help a group solve problems and do good work.

Everything you do is a vote for the world you want. Especially when the thing you do is vote.

"Thank goodness you're here!"

Handy templates

I've made a few spreadsheets you can adapt or just use as inspiration to create and manage your list of contacts, keep a basic campaign calendar, and create a communications plan that keeps you on track to deliver your key election campaign messages.

You can find these free downloads at
www.suzycooper.com.au

Of course, if you're not a spreadsheet kind of person, do what works for you – use a digital calendar, online project management software, or stick post-its and bits of string to your wall the way TV-show detectives do.

Good luck!

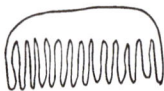

Did someone lend you this book?

If someone lent you this book, they're an excellent person. They obviously think you're someone who could make some great decisions and help all kinds of new voices to be heard in our community.

I wrote and paid for the design and publication of this book myself because I wanted to get it out into the world.

I'd love it if you were willing to support my work and buy your own hard copy or digital copy of the book for yourself or a friend. You'll help me to cover my costs and reach even more people so they can make a difference where they live.

Suzy

"Thank goodness you're here!"

Want some help with your campaign?

It's hard to do it all alone. Sometimes you need a sounding board and your friends and family all get the same glazed look when you start talking about your campaign.

I'm here to help if you want a cheery, straight-talking collaborator to:

- find your points of difference
- work out your key message/s
- identify your potential voters and decide how you'll talk to them.

Visit my website to book a free, zero-obligation introductory chat and decide whether you'd find a few sessions with me valuable.

It can be a relief to get clear about what you're going to do (and not going to do).

Go well!

www.suzycooper.com.au

"Thank goodness you're here!"